Money from Antiques

Milan Vesely

Published by

 **krause
publications**

700 E. State Street • Iola, WI 54990-0001
Telephone: 715/445-2214

Please call or write for our free catalog.
Our toll-free number to place an order or obtain a free catalog is 800-258-0929
or please use our regular business telephone 715-445-2214
for editorial comment and further information.

Library of Congress Catalog Number: 95-82417
ISBN: 0-87341-441-1
Printed in the United States of America

Photo credit: Gerry Grazulis of Photo Grazulis, Grapevine, Texas

Contents

Acknowledgments

I wish to acknowledge the help of many wonderful and knowledgeable people in the preparation of this book. Without my wife, Ruth, the "Lamp Lady" Beverly Fryhover, Anne Slade, Bill Guest, and Pat, Alan, Jeff, and Terry in England, this book would not have been possible.

1. Is the Antique Business for You?

"I have my own antique business."

How many of us have heard those words with envy? Do the words "antique business" conjure up excitement, the vision of an interesting job, and the thought of a good income?

You are not alone. Thousands and thousands of dealers feel the same way! In fact, just by dreaming of financial independence and control over your working life, you already have the single most important asset required to succeed. Your dream is far more important than money or ability. Never forget it, even when you are feeling low—then you will succeed.

And the risks?

Not that great, when you consider the rewards.

"But I have no idea how to start," you say.

Don't worry, you already have. By reading this chapter you have taken the first step in realizing your dream. I will help you. All my experience, the success that I have had, and the "tricks of the trade" that I have learned, are detailed in subsequent chapters. With this information and your ability, you have every chance of making your dream come true. All you have to do is make the decision to start.

So, feel good about yourself. Go for it! Have fun and make yourself some money.

"How much?"

Low five figure profits are certainly normal for a good two booth operation, and six figures are not unheard of with multiple booths.

"Wow!"

Sound good? You can achieve the same. Like you, millions of us want to better ourselves, be independent, and feel a sense of achievement. This nation was brought up in the belief that we can succeed in anything that we desire if we are prepared to work hard for it.

This, of course, is true.

Why do most of us hesitate to take the plunge then?

Because of fear—fear of failure, fear of ridicule, and even fear of coming out of our comfortable shell by taking a risk. Welcome to the club. You are not alone. This is completely natural and happens to every one of us.

The thing you have to remember is that you have unique, individual abilities that make you someone special. If utilized properly, they will guarantee your success in the antique business. To illustrate this, I would like to tell you about my friend Kathy who used to work for me.

By nature, Kathy is a very unsure person. The wife of a high-powered auto executive, she had never taken risks; she never had to. As a result, she hesitated every time she had to give a customer a discount to close a sale, even though I had given her the authority to do so. Her hesitancy cost us business.

While working for me she got inspired, took the plunge, and opened her own booth in a nearby mall. At first she was so cautious in her buying of merchandise that she only purchased cheap, low-end items. The result? She made no profit.

Bit by bit she gained confidence. She got bolder, took more chances, and bought more expensive items, but she never lost her concern for each and every penny. The very traits that made it difficult for her to work for me, proved perfect in her own business. I will never forget the glow on Kathy's face when she made her first decent profit. She could be you!

At the other end of the scale is Jeanie. Always bubbling, always confident, she is a perennial ball of fire. I enjoyed her visits because she usually bought my better merchandise. One evening I met her in a restaurant.

"Guess what?" she said, "I've been so inspired by you, that I've started my own antique business in a nearby mall and I'm having a terrific time!" The airline business lost a flight attendant and the antique world gained a wonderful dealer. Welcome Jeanie!

If my friends Kathy and Jeanie can do it, so can you. Go for it!

Now all you need is knowledge. In the following pages, I will detail my experiences, failures, and most of all, the knowledge that I gained over many years. It will help you to succeed, but first I would suggest that you get yourself a motto. Think of what you really desire, write it boldly on a piece of paper as a daily reminder, and then let it inspire you.

I have my own motto:

I *am* going to travel first class!

$$\$ \ \$ \ \$ \ \$ \ \$$

So why the antique business?

Since most of us have limited financial resources, starting or buying a main street business is beyond our reach. It requires too much cash, too much risk, too much knowledge, and too large a commitment of time.

The antique business does not. It only requires that you have the will to act on your dream, are prepared to do a little work, and have a minimum amount of capital.

I will supply the know-how, and I promise to do so in fun language that you and I both understand, and not in the technical jargon used by professionals to befuddle us. After all, how many of us are CPAs with a Harvard degree?

To understand how the antique business differs from others, I will have to go back a bit and explain how it evolved. There are valuable lessons to be learned from this, not because they are exciting, but because the market forces that caused a proliferation of antique malls in all the major cities are still there. These forces will have both a positive and negative effect on your business in the future. In the following chapters I will explain them and advise you how to use them to your best advantage.

As most people are aware, the building frenzy of the late 1980s left banks and developers holding many empty buildings. They were empty because the amount of available retail space exceeded demand.

Unable to find tenants with deep pockets willing to rent large store space, the developers came up with a very smart idea. Instead of leasing the spaces to one tenant, they turned them into malls and let smaller spaces to multiple tenants. At an average cost of $250 per month for a ten foot booth, it brought retail space within reach of thousands and thousands of budding entrepreneurs. As this snowballed, more and more building owners did the same. It became almost a franchise business. It also spawned whole new categories of businesses as importers, auctioneers, and refinishers rushed in to supply demand.

Most antique malls now advertise, handle all sales, pay the taxes, and staff the whole operation for you. All you have to do is to buy your own merchandise, set up your booth to best advantage, and collect the bimonthly sales check. Of course it's not as easy as that!

While the malls draw in the customers, the secret of your success will depend on how you take advantage of the people they attract, and how you build up your own following.

Hopefully, the advice I offer and the know-how I impart will help you. Use it, throw away what doesn't apply to you, and remember, nothing is set in concrete.

A word of caution is in order here: the property cycle is repeating itself. I believe that the antique malls are in danger of falling into the same trap as the original developers, i.e. too many malls chasing too little business. In later chapters, I will explain how to choose your location to ensure that you don't find yourself looking at a "Gone Out of Business" sign while your goods are still locked inside.

$ $ $ $ $

Okay. So you want to know if the retail antique business is for you?

Here are some basic questions to ask yourself. I will list them all first, and then follow up with further details.

---

1. Is my dream of owning my own small business strong enough to overcome my desire to watch the Sunday afternoon football game? Already I can hear the groans! Come on, come on! Remember your motto.
2. Am I prepared to do five hours extra work each week to run my booth while earning a good second income, or twenty hours more to earn a living wage?

3. Do I have $2000 to $3000 to invest, without it bankrupting me?
4. Will my spouse share in this endeavor?
5. Do I have the patience to do the necessary paperwork every month to ensure that I know the state of my business?
6. Do I have the temperament not to worry all the time?
7. Am I capable of taking a risk occasionally?
8. Am I flexible?
9. Do I have a sense of humor?
10. Do I have a positive outlook?

Before you answer the above questions, I will elaborate on them a little. For this to be useful to you, I will explain both the positive and the negative aspects involved in each question. Hopefully, in answering the above questions you will also learn something about yourself.

1. *Remember Sunday afternoon football games?*
   The busiest days in the antique business are Saturdays and Sundays. You must be prepared to work on weekends. Not necessarily all weekends, but certainly a large number of them. I remember finalizing a large furniture sale during one of the most important Dallas Cowboys games. The lady in question had left her couch potato husband watching the game and closed the sale in a fit of rebellion at his preoccupation with football. I often wonder if he even noticed us delivering it the next Sunday. The blaring television drowned out our conversation and all I ever saw of him was the back of his head above the couch.

2. *Only five hours extra work per week.*
   Easy you say. This doesn't sound like much, but consider that you will have to do this after a full day's work unless you're retired. Getting your feet up and having a beer or a glass of wine will be very tempting after a rough day and a dressing down from your boss. Just remember, if you want to tell him or her to "Take this job and shove it," you will have to go and check on your booth.

3. *Spending $2000 to $3000.*

Booth space and inventory cost money. Depending on the size of your booth and the quality of merchandise, the figures mentioned will be a minimum requirement. If you start your own store, you will need at least fifty to one hundred thousand dollars. Do thoughts of that disappearing vacation suddenly fill your head?

The best advice I can give you to make this pill easier to swallow, is to remember my motto: "I am going to travel first class!" Think of how much fun it will be next year when you don't have to travel in the cheap seats.

4. *Partners sharing—also called sweat-shop labor.*

This is extremely important. Unless your spouse shares in your endeavor it could cause a rift. More often than not however, it causes a closer bonding. In one antique co-op that I know of, the husband and wife teams have a great party together once a month during which they share experiences. ***Mucho fun for all!***

In any case, you will need help moving furniture, and what's more cost effective than a volunteer worker?

5. *Paperwork—a reality check.*

If you are like me you will hate paperwork, but it is essential for you to know the state of your business. Figures don't lie, so like a root canal, they are a necessary evil. However, since you are using your smarts and my advice in running your business, I can already see the ear-to-ear smile on your face as you study the figures on the bottom line. No red ink here!

6. *Do you worry or have nerves of steel?*

To run your own business it helps to be philosophical. The retail business has ups and downs and you must be able to keep your eye on the overall picture and not worry during quiet periods. This is easier said than done, but worrying takes the fun out of earning all that extra cash. Be positive … think of how much money you will make when the buying frenzy starts again next month!

7. *Risk taking — Profit and fun?*

I'm not a great risk taker, you say. I worry too much. Nonsense! You're a fun person, aren't you? When done carefully, taking a risk can be most satisfying and profitable. When I talk of taking a risk, I don't mean being irresponsible. **I mean purchasing something out of the ordinary that someone will buy from you sooner or later at a huge profit.** Sometimes this leads to developing a very profitable niche market for yourself.

You must also occasionally risk marking up an item at double your normal profit. It will surprise you when it flies off the shelf.

Example: I once bought a small copper boiler used to make steam for antique toy trains. It was too expensive, totally useless, and I thought that only a cuckoo-crazy engineer would buy it. A young lady paid $900 for it. She wanted to impress her boyfriend. Ever since then, I buy strange items for those looking to impress someone special.

8. *Flexibility — Nothing is definite.*

The most effective way to maximize profits is to use your knowledge of the market to vary your mark-up. **Popular items should be priced so that they sell fast at smaller profit margins,** keeping in mind that this will help cash flow.

Example: I sell thirty six-dollar table lamps at less then double cost, but sell a very unusual table, buffet, and chair set at five times what I paid for it.

9. *A sense of humor is essential because human beings are the strangest creatures on God's earth.*

You need a sense of humor in this business to understand why some people will think you are too expensive, some too cheap, and most that you must already be a millionaire. Can you laugh at yourself? It'll make you a better person and a better antique dealer at the same time. You'll also enjoy it more.

10. *"I am going to travel first class." How's that for positive?*

A positive outlook is essential or you'll get ulcers. Remember that it's supposed to be fun as well as profitable.

In any case, *customers buy from confident sales people* and hesitate if you look like the sky's about to fall down.

In the following chapters I will share with you my successes, failures, and all that I have learned in running my own successful antique business. It will help you to succeed.

"But I know nothing about antiques," you say with a last procrastinating gasp.

The secret is that you don't have to! All you have to do is to read the chapters on getting started, merchandise, setting up, costing, etc.

So ... is it for you?

If you are working or retired, have a few hours a week, laugh a lot, and have nerves of steel, it is for you! Successful antique dealers are made, not born. They come from all walks of life and from all social backgrounds. The risk is minimal and the rewards can be great.

Try it!

It is for you!

Getting Started

You've made the decision, have the money, and are now itching to get started. This is going to be fun … you can't wait!

Slow down. Control your enthusiasm.

"What's that," you ask, "slow down?"

From my observations, **more mistakes are made and more money lost in the initial surge of excitement** than I care to remember, and I don't even want to think of the blunders I've made. **Take your time, use your head, and you'll start on the right footing**. If you don't believe me, try this test.

When you go to your next party, look around at all the people in the room as you enter. Remember those that attract you, the ones you'd like to meet. During the evening, go up to the beautiful people that you picked and talk to them. You'll be surprised at how many turn out to be disappointments. The point is, first appearances are never what they seem to be.

"What's this got to do with antiques?"

Just this. That piece of furniture, the empty booth the mall owner is pushing to rent, or that pile of specially discounted glassware, just don't seem the same bargain once the deed is done. It is better to sleep on it. They'll still be there tomorrow.

"So what do I do?"

Write yourself a list and gather information. The more information you can dig up, the better. Remember me saying that successful dealers are made, not born? This is the difference between good and bad ones. **All successful dealers base their decisions on facts, not on enthusiasm**. If you can do this coldly and logically, you are almost assured of success. Keep just a touch of that enthusiasm alive, and you will make money **and** have fun.

"What kind of list? What kind of information?" you want to know.

Before I give you my suggested list, let's first consider a few questions.

1. *Do I want to do it part-time or full-time?*

   I recommend that all newcomers initially enter the business part-time. You can always increase your involvement later as your learning curve goes up. It will be cheaper and the initial risk smaller.

2. *Do I want to operate my antique business from home or rent a booth?*

   Give yourself a chance … **rent a booth**. You need the instant traffic and the rent is no more than you'd spend on advertising if you operated out of your home.

3. *Which location?*

   Follow these steps in deciding the best location for your business: 1) Get yourself a local map of your town or city. Draw a five to ten mile circle centered on your house. 2) Get your yellow pages and mark in all the antique shops and malls within or just outside the circle. Note their groupings. The more in one area the better. 3) Using a different colored pen, mark in the main roads and note which malls are the closest to these. 4) Changing color again, shade in all the major residential areas. 5) With the above information, list the shops and malls that have easy access (main roads), are located in groups (draw more customers), and are situated near large residential areas (captive customer base). 6) Go visit each and every one of them. This is the beginning of the fun part and can be most satisfying, because if you do it properly you will learn a lot about yourself, gain confidence, and begin to act like the professional you will become.

I cannot emphasize enough that if you consciously establish your goals, work hard, and use the smarts that you have, you will succeed. Trust me!

You will also gain respect. You do want respect, don't you?

Yes? Then just imagine how proud you will be when your friends or other dealers find out that you take a professional approach to your new business, instead of just rushing in blindly like ninety-five percent of the beginners do.

Well done! You've harnessed your drive and know-how to achieve your desire.

$ $ $ $

Okay, enough of the self-congratulations. Back to work.

When establishing which mall or location is best for you, I recommend that trusty checklist that I mentioned earlier. It will help you professionally decide which one gives you the best chance of success, and since you have everything written down, you can leisurely peruse it at home. It will also enable you to remember various likes and dislikes.

Here is my suggested list:

1. Was this location easy to get to from home?	Yes/No
2. Can it be clearly seen from the approach road?	Yes/No
3. Is it easily accessible?	Yes/No
4. Is there plenty of parking available?	Yes/No
5. Is the building attractive?	Yes/No
6. Is it welcoming as you enter?	Yes/No
7. Does someone greet you?	Yes/No
8. Is it well lit?	Yes/No
9. Does it look busy? (Go at 11 a.m. or 4 p.m.)	Yes/No
10. Is it clean?	Yes/No
11. Are at least eighty percent of the booths full?	Yes/No
12. Are the booths professionally set up?	Yes/No
13. Is the merchandise in the booths of good quality?	Yes/No
14. Does it look high-end?	Yes/No
15. Does it look low-end?	Yes/No
16. Are there a lot of discounted or marked-down prices?	Yes/No

17. Are the counter staff cheerful and attentive?	Yes/No
18. Is there a tea/coffee shop or restaurant?	Yes/No
19. Are hand carts or baskets available?	Yes/No
20. Did booth holders have good things to say?	Yes/No
21. Listen to customer comments. Were they good?	Yes/No
22. Is there a bulletin board?	Yes/No
23. Does management hold sales events?	Yes/No
24. How long has the place been open? Over two years?	Yes/No

As you will see, I have used a simple Yes/No system. It will make it easier to check off the answers as you walk around the malls and save you the embarrassment of having security coming up to you and asking you to leave!

Now you can start to short-list the locations that give you the best chance of success. It will help you to decide what quality merchandise you should carry (#13), what price points to sell at (#14, 15), and what pricing policy you will have to follow (#16). It will also give you the first extra sales outlets (#22 and 23). In addition, you can feel more comfortable, as you are not likely to see that "Gone Out of Business" sign. Remember it? Since many new businesses close within two years, question #24 will ease your mind.

Most important, however, it means that you just might see the end of that important football game on any given Sunday if you hurry (#1).

So! Easy, isn't it? That's what they tell you in those get-rich-quick programs on television. Of course it isn't. But you now have a plan and a direction which, if you are like me, helps you get started by taking the mystery out of it. Go ahead then, sign a lease on your first place of business.

Feels great, doesn't it? You've done well.

$ $ $ $ $

Good choice! You are now the future owner of your own antiques retail location. Things went well. The mall owner was so nice! Why, he even agreed to give you one week's free rent to get set up.

What? You didn't ask him? I didn't tell you to?

Ah well! ... even I'm fallible. I promise not to forget again.

$ $ $ $ $

You have the booth. Now you need to fill the space.

"How? Where do I find the merchandise?"

Stop worrying. Remember that trusty map on which you drew the five or ten mile circle? And the yellow pages? Well, you already have the first source of supply lined up because you have all the dealer's locations marked. Now all you have to do is use the yellow pages and, with a different colored pen, **mark in all the auction houses in your area**. You've already got all the residential areas in, so you also know where all the **garage sales** are likely to be.

See what you are doing? You are developing an **information board** with all supply sources marked in. You also have another income possibility.

"How's that?"

Sometime in the future, when that customer asks you for a pink lamp, you will know where to get one because you will know where you saw one. Either that, or you can ask the booth owner to give you a commission and direct the customer to his or her business. You want that extra money, don't you? You will also have some early evening and weekend entertainment because now is the time to call all the auction houses, find out the time and place of their regular auctions, and ask them to put you on their mailing lists. *Voila!* You have another ready supply of merchandise. That's three already—other dealers discounting items, auctions, and garage sales—and you've only just begun.

All you need now is a few good **flea markets**! Go ask around. Other dealers will tell you where to find them locally.

Oh, and **estate sales** are advertised in the paper in case you didn't know.

I know that's a lot to remember, but don't worry, it'll get easier. It's like riding a bicycle. Practice makes perfect.

So! Let's recap what we have learned.

Chapter 2 review

1. **Stay cool.** When getting started, slow down! More mistakes are made at this early stage than at any other

time. Remember, things are not always what they seem to be at first glance.

2. **Give yourself a fighting chance.** Rent a booth in a well-run, busy mall. It's the best way. Use the checklist to select one.

3. **You have your map.** Or is it an information board? Use it to network with other dealers and gain extra income (remember the pink lamp?). That extra commission will sure help at the end of the month. Update your information board regularly and use it to expand into your second booth, third, or maybe more? It will stand you in good stead through all the years that you will be involved in antiques.

4. **You have developed your own mall rating system.** Use it occasionally to check on the one you're in, particularly when your booth contract comes up for renewal. There may be a better business location in your area.

5. **Where to buy merchandise?** Your data-filled information map will have everything at a glance. Expand this with a supplementary list and you will have all needed phone numbers, regular auction dates, possible garage sales, etc. It will save you scrambling around with a phone book when you're in a hurry.

$$\$ \; \$ \; \$ \; \$$$

Okay. Read on. We're going to take the mystery out of antiques.

"Thank goodness!" you say, "I don't know anything about them and those dealers talk about Barley twist, draw-leaf tables, and halltrees as if they are some exotic product. It makes me feel inadequate."

Don't worry. By the time we finish, you'll run circles around ninety percent of them. I promise.

3. Antiques — What Does This Mean?

What is an antique?

A very good question. Legally, both in the United States and internationally, an antique is any item over one hundred years old. In many countries today you cannot export a one hundred-year-old antique without special permits, and these are almost impossible to obtain. Governments in Europe in particular are concerned that their national heritage and treasures are being plundered and will be lost to them forever.

But does this concern you?

The answer is NO. Not unless you intend to import your own antiques from elsewhere and I will cover that in more detail in Chapter 5 when I deal with buying overseas, importing, and shipping. While it is a good idea to know a little about seventeenth, eighteenth, and nineteenth century antiques, it will have very little bearing on the average dealer's business.

"So what should I know about antiques?"

Well, since you want to be considered a reputable dealer, you need to know what the industry standard is. After all, having started in a professional manner, it would be a shame not to build on your growing reputation, wouldn't it?

Knight's purse. A genuine and unusual antique.

1880 Georgian bookcase. Since a genuine, unusual antique is a one-of-a-kind, no one can compare your price on the same product elsewhere.

Setting your standards

The norm used today in the retail antique business is that any item manufactured before 1940 is considered a genuine antique. This covers furniture, accessories, glassware, and almost anything else.

"Aha!"

I hear your exclamation. You have just remembered those reproduction chairs in the booth two sections down from yours, and I must admit that if I were you, I would do exactly the same. Unfortunately, in an industry as unregulated as ours, people's imaginations know no bounds, particularly where money is concerned. In many malls today, everything from out-and-out junk to reproduction furniture from Indonesia, modern day Russian crystal, or copies of old master prints are being passed off as antiques. This is a shame, because it does the whole industry an injustice. It also does something else that is even more important to us all.

"What's that?"

It depresses prices, because despite what most people think, the buying public is not gullible. Customers soon learn that the repro chairs an antique dealer is trying to pass off as Victorian can be bought at the neighborhood furniture discounters at prices considerably lower, since they buy them in volume.

But I'm not here to moralize. I am here to help you succeed by maximizing your profit on every sale. Therefore, I give to you the following recommendations:

French dumbwaiter. Be the only professional antique dealer able to find such an unusual gem.

- **Avoid reproductions or modern products** that, because they are mass produced, can almost certainly be found in other stores. The competition will force you to discount them to such an extent that you will make little or no profit. It will also harm your growing reputation while tying up capital that can be used on more profitable and faster selling merchandise.

Now here is the obvious secret:

- **Buy genuine 1940 or older antiques that are unusual.** I repeat—genuine and unusual.

You're too smart to ask why, but humor me. Let me state the obvious.

Since a genuine, unusual antique is a one-off (British for one-of-a-kind), no one can compare your price on the same product elsewhere. Therefore, you can charge more, hold your price, and sell it to the customer that falls in love with it and simply cannot find it anywhere else.

Isn't it a fabulous feeling to make a bigger profit, satisfy a customer's desire, and gain their admiration for being the only professional dealer able to find such an unusual gem?

In my own case, I'll never forget the cheerful lady that paid me $500 for that very special chest. She had seen it in my shop, balked at the price, and hunted for it elsewhere for two long, tiring days. When I loaded it into her trunk, her smile at getting a genuine, unusual antique, almost matched mine at the thought of the paltry $120 I had paid for it.

Now here's a wonderful thought for you. I hope that you will become a professional dealer, selling unusual and genuine products to terrific people, while making yourself a handsome profit. It will satisfy you both.

1760 chatelaine. Sell unusual and genuine products to terrific people while making yourself a handsome profit.

Furniture

European or American? It doesn't matter. What matters is your two criteria—genuine and unusual. Add a third ... pretty. With these three, you can't go wrong.

"Can I mix European and American?"

Sure you can! You're trying to satisfy as wide a range of customers as you can, aren't you?

To help you make decisions on what to actually stock in your booth, just remember your home. The dining room has a table and chairs, a buffet, and a large mirror. The bedroom? A bed, two side

Buffet with Barley twist legs

tables, and a wardrobe. Try to set up your booth in the same manner. Coordinate the furniture. Nothing looks worse than a mish-mash of unrelated items. I'm not just telling you this so that you look professional. I'm telling you this so that you make money. That's what I promised to do.

Think of it like this: If the customer buys the table and chairs, she might also buy the matching buffet and get rid of her old one.

Wouldn't it be great to clear out your whole stock in one go? Maybe she'll even buy the mirror, the set of Worcester plates, and the silver cutlery that you so attractively set out on the table. And how about those antique candlesticks on either end? Wouldn't they look great for her dinner party this Saturday?

Get the picture?

So! Now you have rented your own booth, know where to buy suitable furniture, and even have a plan to coordinate your product range.

Well done! Feel good about yourself. You are on your way to being a successful antique furniture dealer.

Before leaving this section, I will cover some well-known phrases and explain what they mean. This list is by no means complete, but it is enough for you to get started.

Barley twist: Probably the best known description. Almost anyone who is trying to impress you that they are well versed in antiques will quote this one. All it means is that the wood is twisted in swirls. It originated in England and is most commonly seen on table legs, chair legs, and buffet legs. Probably came about because it looks like twisted barley sheaves.

Buffet: Also called a **sideboard**. Food was served off of them in the old days. Now used for the same reason or for storage of tableware, tablecloths, and decorative accessories.

Halltree: A tall (six to seven foot) hat/coat rack, usually comes with a mirror. They generally have six hat hooks on them, as well as side holders for umbrellas and a drip tray on either side. Some have seat chests in the center for storing shoes or boots. Others have a small key box.

Draw-leaf table: Table with side sections that pull out to extend the table's length. Usually seat four to six.

Drop-leaf table Table with sides that drop down when stored. Folded legs come out to hold the leaves up.

Gateleg table: Same as above but usually prettier. Legs swing out sideways like a gate.

Wardrobe: English. Used to store clothes, as they didn't have built-in closets in the old days. Now used in America as entertainment centers. For my English friends—the Americans put stereos, TVs, and VCRs in them.

Dumbwaiter: Same as a buffet but in two or more tiers. Buffets generally have mirrors in the center and dumbwaiters do not.

Halltree. A tall (six to seven foot) hat/coat rack.

"Okay! So what kind of accessories?" you ask.

That's enough to get you started. The rest you will learn as you go. I'll reveal a little secret here. **When talking to customers, say the phrases in a clear, positive voice**. They will think you are a real expert. It always amazed me how few people actually knew what they meant. Just like name-dropping at a party, isn't it? Everyone thinks you are stretching the truth but it still leaves an impression.

Enough about furniture. You now know enough to handle this aspect with confidence. A good way to learn more is to listen to the auctioneers as they hustle to sell a piece. They describe each item in detail to promote the furniture they are selling.

Accessories

Have you ever bought a new car? Most of us have at one time or another. Cast your mind back to that time. Remember how the salesman avoided talking about anything other than the base price until you confirmed that you would buy it, then how all of a sudden, all he could talk about was the great air-conditioning, extended warranty, special wheels, and lovely pinstripes that you absolutely had to have? You do? Well, think of accessories in the same way.

Accessories are the merchandise with which you maximize your profit.

Just think of it this way: You have a captive buyer. Their resistance to spending money has gone. They want the buffet, table, or bureau they bought to look as good in their home as it does in your booth. So why not sell them the candlesticks as well to satisfy this desire?

"Okay, so what kind of accessories?" you ask.

Candlesticks, pictures, table runners, decorative teapots, silverware, tableware, clocks, etc. The list is endless. Anything old, decorative, or functional will do. But just remember this: **When buying accessories, coordinate the products so that they not only sell in their own right as a wonderful item that the customer simply cannot do without, but so that they also help you to sell other products**.

I will give you an example:

You went to the auction last night and bought a great-looking French dining table as well as a beautiful English secretary (looks like a bookcase bureau). You paid a little more for them than you would have liked, but shoot, they're great pieces! Trouble is, you've only got $150 with you at the flea market today instead of your usual $250.

Just then you come up to two side-by-side booths. On one is a terrific, heavy-gilt, framed picture of water lilies. It would look absolutely great on the peach colored left-side wall of your booth. On the other is a pair of ornate French silver candlesticks in very good condition, sitting next to three bound volumes of *The Life of Sir Winston Churchill*. The picture costs $139 and the candlesticks, together with the books, cost $145.

Which should you buy today?

Before you answer that question, remember what I said separated successful dealers from amateurs?

Terrific! Coldly and logically you bought the candlesticks and books. They will decorate, and maybe sell with, the table and secretary. The picture will have to wait for another day.

I'm very proud of you. Your professionalism is beginning to show. You are learning quickly.

Collectibles

Wonderful products. The very word means a captive buying public. Not many antique categories can echo that boast! But what are collectibles? And are they for you?

Let's deal with the first question first. Flow Blue china, Dresden figurines, thimbles, walking sticks, Depression glass, corkscrews, egg beaters, porcelain juice squeezers, teapots, inkwells, perfume bottles, majolica ceramics, pens, purses, golf clubs, etc. The list is endless and growing more so each day. It never ceases to amaze me what people collect. I guess it's a reflection of each of us seeking individuality.

So which should you buy and sell? Obviously the most popular collectibles: Flow Blue china, Depression glass, and perfume bottles are the most sought after. Majolica ceramics are also up there with the best of them.

"So how do I learn what to look for in these products?"

You go to the library, photocopy all the sections dealing with the collectible you have chosen to carry in your booth, and then **study everything about them**. Being smart, you will also talk to as many dealers as possible and attend any shows in your area.

This brings me to the question, "Are collectibles for you?"

The answer is … NO.

Not unless you are already an expert and have been a collector yourself. Certainly not as a beginning dealer.

Why?

Because they are too specialized.

Specialized products are usually overpriced, have too narrow a customer base, and are bought by people that want them at the cheapest possible price. As enthusiasts, they will spend hours on a Saturday afternoon talking to you about the hobby that fascinates them. Without being rude, you would be better advised to go over to the lady with the gold Rolex admiring that pretty secretary that you bought at the auction the other night, and that you have decorated with those three volumes of *The Life of Sir Winston Churchill*.

Collectibles are wonderful products, but you have risked your money and that irritating ulcer to succeed, not to develop new friendships when you should be selling your heart out!

You don't think I'm right? I did say that nothing is set in concrete, but please believe me, I have your best interests at heart.

As a beginning dealer, leave collectibles alone at first. Later, it's a different story.

Glassware

Glassware is a very fast-selling product line and one that I highly recommend that you carry. Old crystal vases, decanters, inkwells, and drinking glasses are excellent sellers. Cobalt blue glass items, if you can get them, will fly off your shelf.

"Why is that?"

Because they are both an impulse buy and a gift item, with the added advantage that they are generic. Everyone can use them. Just remember what you bought as a wedding gift, birthday gift, or anniversary gift, and the chances are that it was a vase, ashtray, or set of glasses. Everyone likes them, and everyone is pleased to get them. You don't have to think too much to make a decision and glassware always looks so terrific that no one will call you a cheapskate.

Vases, wine glasses, condiment sets, punch bowls, and liquor decanters—crystal or cut glass—all are great. You can't buy enough of them and they will always sell.

That's the upside. Now here's the downside: When buying glassware, just remember what I told you at the beginning of this chapter. People are even selling modern reproduction furniture and Russian crystal as antique. Just remember that you are an antique dealer, and follow the basic rules I suggested. If it's old, pre-1940 if possible, but not necessarily so, unusual, and pretty, it will sell.

There is one more standard I think is absolutely essential in building your reputation as a professional dealer which particularly applies to glassware. It is quality.

Always buy and sell quality glassware. Nothing cheapens the look of your professionally set up booth more than chipped and cracked glassware. It instantly transforms you from a knowledgeable, professional antiques dealer … to a junk seller!

So, NO chips, cracks, or broken glass to be seen anywhere, right?

"What if it's been repaired?"

Only if it's a professional repair and the piece is a very, very, unusual and almost rare item. Then, and only then, can you bend the rules ever so slightly. Otherwise no, no, no!

> To summarize glassware:
>
> An excellent, fast, and profitable selling accessory when in first class condition. Crystal and cut glass vases, decanters, and other products are generic impulse items bought by a wide range of customers. Put as much glassware into your booth as possible, but display it all together to make a statement.

You are getting more comfortable with this antique business, aren't you? I can see it.

Special items

Special items make you special profits. Adding them to your business can also be extremely satisfying, as they allow you to express your wonderful personality.

Does that sound strange to you?

I can hear you saying, "But you told us to be coldly logical in everything we do to become a professional."

Of course I did. But I also told you that the antique business

Special items can be great sellers, make you "fabuloso" profits, let your personality run wild, and be great fun to buy and sell.

can be fun and profitable at the same time. Everything in moderation will make you a well-rounded person.

Special items can be great sellers, make you fabuloso profits, let your personality run wild, and be great fun to buy and sell. They can also make you just another junk dealer! Unless you deal in … ?

Quality!

Remember the golden rules: If it's an antique, unusual, pretty, and of good quality, it's a sure bet!

> To help you, I want to mention a few items that I always buy if I come across them: Old wrought-iron gates, crucifixes, antique cash registers, hair brush sets, antique hand mirrors, wooden card boxes, candelabras, sconces, barometers, hydrometers (for measuring liquid density), silver spoons, jewelry boxes, framed historic documents, ashtrays, quilts, rugs, medals, swords, walking sticks, carving sets, and even wooden ship's wheels, to name a few.

Also buy the very unusual. Remember the toy train boiler that I mentioned in Chapter 1? The one I sold for $900? It was so different that someone was prepared to pay for its uniqueness.

Special accessory items

Another item I remember well is the pipestand and tobacco jar combo that I bought. After cleaning the jar, filling it with sugar and putting a silver spoon on the pipestand, I marked it up and sold it at a good price, in fact selling two pieces at one time.

Since I'm now revealing all my secrets, I may as well tell you about the tray and stand a very close friend and partner of mine bought. The tray was a French gilt, scalloped edged serving tray. The stand was also gilt, but was missing whatever had been on top of it originally. Since both were bits 'n' pieces, she got them for a song at a flea market. After we glued the tray to the top of the stand, we sold it for $250 as a lovely occasional table.

So remember to use your imagination. It's probably better than mine and it can help you to make those extra profits. Here are some more suggestions.

> Don't buy:
>
> Old wagon wheels, signs, saddles, bottles, or farm implements. Modern houses simply don't use worn out rural products as decorative additions. Having said don't buy them, there are exceptions. Later on I will cover decorative products used in restaurants and these will be suitable for this aspect of your business.

In concluding this section I would like to wish you success. Let your personality run wild within the criteria of the golden rules. Have fun with these products. They can be very, very profitable. Just no junk, okay?

Books

I love old books. Yellowed, leather-bound, and smelly, they make great accessories. No one ever reads them; not when sold as an antique. But as a decorative piece for that secretary, bookcase, or entry halltree, they really make a statement.

"How do I know what to buy?"

You buy old books printed before 1940 for $30 or less and leave the expensive historic books alone.

"But why?" you say.

Since ninety-five percent of you will not be interested in selling antique books as a specialty, but as added income to your furniture and accessory sales, all you are looking for is interesting, well-known stories and anecdote-type books to sell as decorative pieces. Old *Black Beauty, Robin Hood, English Language Prose* and *Hilarious Tales* spring to mind. A great favorite, which is also an excellent seller, is the old leather-bound family Bible. If you don't believe me, walk around six malls and count how many old English family Bibles you find.

Just make sure that they are in good condition and avoid any with torn pages or damaged covers. Remember, they're a decorative, snob-value piece ... not a book.

Other

This section is very easy. Anything goes as long as it is ... you guessed right! Unusual, antique, tasteful, pretty, good quality, and an item that you would be proud to have in your own home.

Chapter 3 review

This has been a long chapter but you have learned a lot. A quick review is in order before we go on to what I consider the most important chapter in the book.

1. **What is an antique?** In most cases anything made before 1940.

2. **What kind of furniture should I buy?** Genuine, unusual pieces that can't be found everywhere. Coordinate your buying to make up a room and not a mishmash of odd pieces. Avoid reproductions if you can.

3. **What kind of accessories?** Match your accessories to the setting you have in the booth at that time. Dining sets need candles, runners, place mats, cutlery, etc. Sell them as add-ons, just like the car dealers.

4. **Collectibles?** Not for you when starting out unless you are already a collector. Too specialized, expensive, and geared to too small a customer base for the beginner. Later maybe, not now.

5. **Glassware?** Highly recommended. An impulse buy, glassware is of interest to a large customer base. Remember what you always buy as a wedding gift, anniversary present, or birthday present? Crystal, good cut glass, and blue cobalt are all good bets. Don't hesitate on glassware; you can't go wrong. As long as it's old, good quality, and not chipped.

6. **Special items.** Another great category. High profits can be made with these items (remember my boiler?). Let your imagination run wild. Have fun and make lots of profit with this type of merchandise. But remember! Follow the golden rules and no junk.

7. **Books.** Good decorative pieces. Don't pay more than $30. Old family Bibles are excellent.

8. **Other.** Anything goes as long as you'd have it in your own home.

$ $ $ $

You've come a long way. Now that you are really serious, know a lot more than when you started, and really believe that successful antique dealers are made and not born, I will cover the single most important aspect of how to succeed.

Before I do, I want to say this.

There's no mystery in antiques. There is obviously a lot more than I've covered, but you are starting out and want to make money right away, so I've provided you with an overview.

My advice?

Stick to basics at first. The fancy stuff will come later.

Turn to the next chapter. It will change how you do business in the future in whatever you try, not just in the antique business.

4. Judging Your Customer Base

This is a most important, if not *the* most important chapter in this antique dealer's bible. If you do nothing else, read, learn, and inwardly digest the information (pearls of wisdom?) that I will cover. Most of it will have almost nothing to do with you becoming a professional antique dealer, but it is invaluable in starting your own business and in ensuring its success.

Sounds like a heavy subject, but don't worry. Even the most serious subjects can be fun, and as far as I remember, we agreed to have fun and make a profit, didn't we? So let's get on with it.

Judging your customer base—what does this mean?

In simple layman's terms it means **find out everything you can about the customers you are selling to in your surrounding area**. How many are there, their marital status, home ownership details, income level, average age, average number of children per family, education level, average number of vehicles per household, etc.

"What!" I hear you say, "All I want to be is an antique dealer with one, two, or maybe three booths."

Not so. You made me a promise to be a professional antique dealer, and as a professional dealer you want to make cold, logical decisions based on facts.

"But I don't know where to find all this information, and I wouldn't know what to do with it even if I did."

Actually it's surprisingly easy to obtain the information, and once you have it, all you have to do is make an intelligent guess about whether your customers are mid-level working people or high-level professionals.

But first, let us think a little, since we want to do this as easily as possible.

Can you remember that map/information board that you now have hanging above the desk on which you do your necessary paperwork? Do you use it often? Good.

Now, taking your yellow pages again, mark in all the grocery stores, furniture stores, large department stores, and specialty stores within the drawn circle.

Next, go visit them. While you are doing so, ask yourself the following:
1. Are they selling quality, relatively expensive products?
2. Are they selling lower end items?
3. Are the furniture stores selling mainly cheap, press-board furniture, or better, and therefore more expensive lines. If you can't tell, ask the salesmen. They like to talk, particularly on a quiet, boring Thursday afternoon when it's hot and they've made no commission.
4. Are there many specialty stores near your chosen mall?
5. Do the grocery stores carry a large selection of gourmet items and special wines, or are they stocked with basic necessities and lots of generic brands?

Aha! I see a gleam in your eye.

Yes, that's right. We are using their larger resources to help us establish whether we should sell better, expensive items or middle-of-the-road merchandise. After all, they have already done their own demographic research. They always do. They have millions to lose, not just your paltry three thousand dollars. You can bet your bottom dollar that they make sure they are offering the appropriate quality and price-point level merchandise for your chosen area.

Is this enough for us to make our own decisions? I think not.

"Why?"

Because I'm an independent, ornery kind of a guy who likes to think that David did slay Goliath. In other words, I like to find out for myself. I also want more information in case I ever advertise, and since I've started on this work now, I may as well get it over with all at once. By the time I'm finished with you, you will be deluged with data. Use what's useful and throw away what's not.

So where do we get all this extremely valuable, semi-valuable, useful, irrelevant, and sometimes totally useless data?

At your local chamber of commerce, newspaper, library, convention center, building permit office, city hall, and coupon-stuffing business, that's where.

Here's an example:

Since I live in Grapevine, Texas, I went to see my local newspaper and asked them for their circulation figures and customer demographics. I did the same with the *Fort Worth Star Telegram*. Oh sure, I had to tell a little white lie, but I did advertise with them later. I really did, I promise.

Anyway, both were able to tell me how many people live in Grapevine, along with their income level and local buying habits. The *Fort Worth Star Telegram* sent me a wonderful demographic map of the area, detailing in brilliant colors the income level of all the surrounding zip code areas. Tying this in with our local coupon advertising company, I was not only able to establish what my customer base was, but also to plan my future advertising into the most productive areas.

Okay ... so now we know that the customers likely to visit your booth are earning 30-40, 40-50 or 50-60 thousand dollars per year, have an average of two children, own their own home, and drive a new BMW.

"How does that help us?"

Well, for a start we are not going to buy that rickety, scratched, draw-leaf table we saw in the auction are we? No. We will buy that pretty, elegant halltree, even if it goes up to $300 during the bidding. After all, that furniture store around the corner was selling ugly reproduction ones at $750, and since ours is a pretty antique unit, we should get at least $725 for it. You don't mind making a $425 profit do you?

Let's take a closer look at why we selected the halltree: First, we know that our customers earn a decent income and demand a better class of product. Since we also found out that the nearby grocery store carries a large selection of gourmet foods, we know that our potential customer likes to consider himself/herself as sophisticated and worldly. The growth of new, expensive housing in our business area means that large entry halls will have to be filled.

Conclusion?

That beautiful, English, high-quality and slightly more expensive halltree is a safer bet than that cheap, rickety $125 draw-leaf table.

I really care that you succeed, and by now I am sure that you understand that I want you to do as much research as possible. Please apply your considerable abilities and then go for it. If more dealers did that, the industry as a whole would be much better off, and I would hear fewer people say, "They've got nothing but a load of junk" when coming out of a mall.

Besides which, I like it that you are beginning to feel more confident. I keep remembering that you might buy me dinner when I'm in your city on my book tour.

Fat chance, you say?

I'll keep hoping!

Tourists—an additional customer base

Depending on where you live and operate your booth, tourists can be a source of considerable extra income. However, since they are out-of-towners, the criteria you use in buying merchandise for your booth does not completely apply to them. For example, they won't buy large items if shipping is difficult or transport charges high; therefore you will only sell them "smalls" as I like to call them. It's an English word meaning accessories.

To find out if your business area has any tourist traffic, call your local city hall or tourist bureau and ask for statistics. You will be surprised at the useful information they'll provide. Don't forget to ask them if you can leave your flyers at their office for visitors to pick up.

"Will they allow me to do that?"

Sure they will. They're supposed to work for you, aren't they?

In our town of Grapevine we have a very active Tourist Convention Bureau. Twice a year Grapevine holds a town festival during which all the merchants' sales increase considerably. Due to my contacts, the tourist bureau featured my antique store in their promotional literature. This is free advertising for me, and

Is this an antique? Ideal for the tourist trade. Genuine, unusual, and small enough that it can be carried on the plane.

I suggest that you try to do the same with your local tourist organization.

"But I only have a booth!"

No you don't. You have a professionally run business. Act like a professional and people will treat you like one. Here's a suggestion:

Ask your local tourist bureau if they would like you to display their brochures in your booth or booths. There you go! You scratch their backs and they'll scratch yours. You'll be surprised how many visitors will be directed by them to your booth. Do the same with the local hotels. Offer to put their brochures in your business premises (never call it a booth), if they will do the same for you.

So, what kind of "smalls" should you stock to cater to this extra, visiting customer base?

First the criteria:

They have to be accessories small enough to be carried on a plane. They have to be unusual, and they have to be genuine antiques (see illustration).

Sound familiar? How about antique crystal, silverware, inkwell sets, English Bibles, French crucifixes, Worcester plates, and pretty English teapots?

I can hear the words already. "That's the normal merchandise you suggested I carry for my regular customers."

Of course it is, but what's different is packaging and psychology.

Let's tackle packaging first. Go buy yourself some very fancy boxes, use pretty wrapping paper and ribbons, have the local printer make up some elegant cards with your business name on them in olde English letters, and hand write a short history of your business on them. Add your tourist bureau literature to each box with the product you are packaging, and you have special merchandise targeted at your tourist customer base. You also have something extra that your regular customers can send to out-of-town relatives.

"But what was that psychology all about?"

To answer that, I will ask you a question first. What is the tourist looking for? A present? A gift? Of course not. The tourist is looking for a pleasant memory or wants to boast to friends in a subtle way.

You heard right. Tourists don't buy presents, they buy memories or show-off items. After all, they can probably get an antique crystal vase in their own hometown.

Think about it. Tourists buy items to remember the wonderful time they had with relatives and to let everyone back home know about it. It is a well-known fact that people spend more on impulse items when on vacation than when they are in their normal 9 to 5 daily grind. So take advantage of it. Make yourself that extra money. It's well worth it.

"How about costs? Can I charge extra?"

You can charge extra for all the packaging, and you can ship UPS, Federal Express, or U.S. Mail and charge extra for that service as well. Handling fee is what many stores call it.

"Wow! I can even take phone orders from customers who have visited my booth."

Yes, but you will have to set all this up in a special corner and have various sizes of boxes made up so that the customer just picks one up, places the item into it, and pays at the mall counter. You will also need a dedicated phone line in your house to take in the orders. Don't forget, you are a professional. Nothing will cause a customer to hesitate in parting with hard earned cash more than if your teenage daughter answers "Yo!" when they call.

You will have to set this arrangement up with the mall owner and ask them if they will do UPS, Federal Express, and U.S. Mail shipping for you. Suggest that you are prepared to pay an additional twenty dollars with your rent for the extra attention that their staff gives to customers wishing to take advantage of your Special Tourist Package. If they're smart, they'll be excited at earning some extra income. They could even offer the service to other booth holders.

Remember the car salesman? The extras have higher profits and don't carry discounts. It is a lot to set up, but once the system's working, it requires very little attention.

Try it. You'll be surprised how much extra you will make.

Using your customer data to the max

Being such a professional, you now have a jump on your competition. You are running your business and making decisions on hard facts. You know whether you should be carrying better class products, medium income level ones, or very high-end specialty antiques. Your tourist section is also doing great. You feel good about yourself, and so you should.

But don't get complacent. Running your own business requires something more.

How about your competition? Are they standing still? Hopefully yes, but they may also have bought this book. And

The point is, they need lamps to go with those night tables they bought from you. Where do they buy them? From you, of course!

your friends Jim and Mary over there are almost as smart as you. Not quite, but almost as smart.

"So what else can I do?"

Use your data and find yourself a large, profitable niche. Note the word large. You never want to carry any products that have a narrow customer base like collectibles. You need to sell to as many people as possible, all the time.

Lamps! Lamps! and more lamps! Specialize in one fast-selling line.

"So give me a clue what I should look for."

How about a range of unique, antique, bedside lamps? Your fifty thousand a year professional accountant, building his new dream home and driving his latest BMW, takes work home to keep up with the corporate rat race. Both he and his wife like to read at night, so they need bedside lamps to go with those night tables they bought from you. Where better to buy them than from you again? Surprise, surprise! You have a collection of them in your booth just itching for a home.

What's the lesson in this?

Specialize in one fast-selling line.

Beverly Fryhover taught me this. She had always been the leader in sales in her co-op. Her partners watched her and developed their own niches—Mary with pictures, Debbie with crystal, and

Darla with greeting cards. Soon their sales matched hers and even surpassed hers. I always remember her worrying about it until she increased her lamp lines. That did it. Soon she was back on top. Guess what she calls herself? The Lamp Lady, of course!

Mirrors, small pictures, and occasional tables are just a few of the items you can specialize in. These items are bought by a large number of customers. By grouping them in a corner you can make a product statement and develop a niche market to get a jump on your competition. Don't forget, you will have to change out your booth regularly to give it a fresh look. These types of products will fit in with your dining room setting, bedroom setting, or your living room arrangement. Remember when we discussed these?

Chapter 4 review

I will now summarize this most important chapter.

As I mentioned at the beginning, use its lessons to the max. If you do, you will become a shrewd, smart businessman or businesswoman, and not just a smart antique dealer.

1. **Find out what your customer base is by getting your local population demographics**. Using their average income level, home ownership details, buying habits, and tastes, purchase and sell merchandise to suit their preferences.

2. **You can obtain all this information** from your city hall, tourist bureau, housing permit department, library, newspapers, and local advertising companies. Newspapers are particularly good sources, as they have tons of information and will gladly give it to you in anticipation of your future advertising.

3. **Get additional information** by visiting the nearby grocery stores (large gourmet sections?), furniture stores (the salesman will tell you if they carry low-, mid- or high-end products and how they are doing), as well as any specialty stores (sophisticated tastes?).

4. **Use these sources to promote your business**. Remember the flyers you are going to leave in the tourist bureau offices and nearby hotels? They work.

5. **Build on your tourist customer base** with special packaging and your amateur psychology training. Use tourist brochures, your own card, and shipping. It helps the tourist customer treasure those happy memories and boast to their friends and relatives unable to come to your wonderful establishment.

6. **Get a jump on your competition**. Using your data, build yourself a broad, customer-based, niche market. Lamps, mirrors, small English country scene pictures, and unusual occasional tables will do it.

$ $ $ $ $

Finally, set all your data down in a written summary. You now have a marketing plan. Clip it up alongside your information board. Update it regularly. Situations change.

Example: In a small town, the largest local employer closes down. Your booth is in the Main Street mall. Very quickly, your local customers stop spending to conserve their cash. At the same time your booth lease is due for renewal. Do you take up that other booth in your mall, or do you move south to the nearby town where the same industry is expanding? It's no further, just a different direction. Using your basic data format (marketing plan), all you have to do is to call the other town's city hall, newspaper, tourist bureau, et al.

You've already done it?

"Yes."

When?

"When I was first contemplating expanding."

Wow! You're going to beat me at my own game. You really are becoming a professional, and a good one at that. Just don't start writing books please.

5. Finding Merchandise

"What kind of merchandise shall I buy to be successful?"

The kind that you would like to have in your own home. What a wonderful guideline. It was said to me by my friend Beverly Fryhover as she explained the intricacies of running a successful antique business. Later I was to learn how accurate her judgment was, and how appropriate those words were. Time and time again she would bring an unusual item into my store, and lo and behold, a short while later it sold.

Where do we find such pretty, unusual, bestsellers that we would like to have in our own home?

At the local antique auctions, at estate sales, at garage sales, from other dealers, from newspaper advertisements, from private sellers, and at flea markets, also called car boot sales in England.

Car boot sales? I can already see the puzzled look on my American friends' faces. In England, the car's trunk is called a boot and it's hood a bonnet. Silly? No more than trunk and hood if you think about it.

You've never been to England?

Well, when you are successful you should treat yourself to a working vacation (called a holiday in England). Since you will be successful, I cover buying antiques overseas briefly in this chapter. See how much faith I have in you?

But enough of the frivolous chit chat. This is serious business. I am supposed to be teaching you special buying techniques, so here's a piece of advice:

Just remember, the biggest asset you have is your intelligence and your ability to stay cool under pressure.

Auctions

Auctions are one of the easiest, although not necessarily the cheapest, sources of supply. But a warning: The very system of bidding is designed to generate excitement and competitive spirit so that the prices keep increasing to the maximum. Add this to the constant scrutiny that you are under when bidding, and you have a situation ripe for a financial disaster. In addition, the auctioneer's prompt man pressures you by staring directly at you when the action slows and plays on your desire not to look foolish. With all this against you, you have very little chance.

That is, unless you are tough and professional.

"So what should I do?"

Give yourself a shock! Think of something that brings you back down to earth.

"Such as?"

I always remember the unsmiling face of the bank manager when I had to ask for an overdraft. It's funny how much he always looks like the prompt man at every auction I attend and how tough it makes me once I reach my decided buying price. Notice I said "decided buying price." This is very important and I will cover it in detail in the chapter on buying merchandise. Suffice to say at this time, that it is my maximum purchase price for that particular piece.

So, recalling that manager's face makes me instantly tough and professional. The prompt man can pressure all he likes, it'll make no difference. If the price is too high, I won't buy it. The ugly manager wins out every time. It works for me. You choose your own mental picture and use it at the appropriate moment.

Finally, do your homework. Go to the early viewing. Be prepared. Take a calculator, pencil, and pad of paper. Then follow these steps:

1. As you walk into the auction room, stop and slowly look around at all the merchandise. Make a mental note of what catches your eye. These are your first choice pieces.

2. Slowly walk around examining any piece that complies with your golden rules. Remember them? Antique, unusual, and pretty. In particular, look at the pieces that first caught your eye as you walked into the room.

3. List these on a piece of paper.

4. Go around again and carefully check the listed pieces for damage, broken hinges, lifting veneer, and any other blemishes. Ignore all other items. You are not interested in them any more.

5. Check the position of the selected pieces so that you can judge when they are likely to come up for auction. The auctioneer will sell small, inexpensive items first to warm up the crowd and loosen their resistance to spending money. Next, he will sell off the items closest to him, working the left and right side alternately. Occasionally he will vary this and start at the back first, but this is more the exception than the rule.

6. I like to sit on the side of the seating rows about three-quarters back. My other favorite spot is to stand in the middle, right at the back, in full view of the auctioneer. I do this so that anyone bidding against me will have a hard time seeing me, but at the same time I am in full view of the auctioneer and his prompt man. It's amazing how intimidated people feel when they can't see their opponent. They just hate turning around to see who's trying to beat them out of that piece.

7. Remember the ugly face of the bank manager and become coldly professional. Stay cool and don't let the prompt man rush you into buying a mistake.

8. Don't bid on the item at first. Let others do the running. Then, when the bidding slows and the auctioneer starts to prompt, make your first bid. You will be surprised how it defeats your other opponent psychologically. He or she has already expended gobs of adrenaline and you coming in now might just make them give up, saving you money. Does this sound like war? Sure. Try it sometime. You'll be surprised at how effective it is.

9. Finally, don't rush to up the bid every time someone else goes higher. Just wait. Remember that the auctioneer's prompt man will give you at least five shots at increasing

the bid before he gives up on you. This technique helps to cast doubt into the other bidder's mind as to the value of the piece, and may save you a few dollars.

10. But most important of all, never, never, go higher than your decided buying price. "Easier said than done," you say. Yes, but this is what separates the pros from the amateurs. Do I ever slip up? Of course I do. Don't feel too bad if you do, but just don't do it too often.

11. Don't forget that you can submit absentee bids at most auctions. All this means is that you can put in a sealed bid if you can't be there physically. If the price reached during the bidding is lower than your bid, you will be the proud owner of the item.

Here are a few tips to bear in mind at auctions:

• If most of the merchandise is low-end junk and there are only a very few good pieces among them—go home. The bidding will go too high because there will be too many dealers after the same piece.

• If the pieces you are interested in bidding on are far apart, get up, go and get coffee, or go to the bathroom and wash your face with cold water. It will make you tough and professional, particularly if you didn't get that last piece.

• Now for a sour note. Some unscrupulous auctioneers raise the bids by having their own people act as buyers. These crooks are few and far between, as most auctioneers are reputable, good and honest businessmen. By watching closely you will be able to detect this, and if you do I suggest you get up and walk out.

• One final thing. Always check the times of the auction beforehand. A very smart friend and I spent hours previewing merchandise, only to find that the auction time had been changed. When she got there, the cupboard was bare, and we missed out on some very nice pieces. We had a great laugh, but it was a very wasted effort.

Have fun! It can be a social outing as well as business. Many people meet their friends and enjoy the day or evening. Just don't forget that you are now a professional. The enjoyment quickly sours when you worry about having paid too much for that desk, table, or porcelain figurine.

I have a motto that helps me avoid that feeling. As soon as the bidding reaches my decided buying price, I say to myself, "If it stinks, don't step in it." It works amazingly well.

I also use that phrase when customers mess around with me.

Let's take a break, and I'll tell you a story to illustrate how effective this phrase has been for me.

I had a customer who gave me an order for thirty tables and two hundred chairs. Yeah! Terrific order. I thought so too. The only snag was that I had to ship in the goods from my English warehouse. Since I had two months to deliver, there was no real problem.

During lunch at my expense, I asked him for a deposit of thirty percent. Suddenly the order became 28 tables and 150 chairs and he would confirm it the next Monday. When he did call me, the order had changed again to 18 tables and no chairs since "someone would sell him the chairs at $30 each,"—$10 below my asking price.

At this stage I remembered "If it stinks, don't step in it." I backed out of the deal. Later I heard that somebody else had supplied the tables at $100 less than me and never got paid. Not only did I not waste my time, but I didn't lose money either.

Estate sales

Almost the same as auction sales but usually with higher caliber merchandise. The other difference is that they often have reserve prices on some of the pieces, if not on all.

The thing I like about estate sales is that they are usually held *in situ*, i.e. in the house where the owner lives. By keeping my eyes open, I very often notice how the other half lives and this helps me when setting up my own booth or store. The rich, in particular, have the expertise of interior decorators to call on and I copy their ideas. Estate sales also keep me up to date on the going price for better merchandise.

When buying at estate sales, all the same rules apply as at auctions. Pinpoint the merchandise you are interested in, check it thoroughly for damage, set your decided buying price, and then act professionally. Most estate sales are advertised in your local paper. Look out for them.

I personally don't buy much at estate sales because the prices are usually higher than elsewhere. I only purchase items for which I can charge double and still add a cushion to cover any future discounts. Occasionally, very occasionally, I find a bargain.

So, are they for you? Definitely yes. Just be careful about paying too much.

Garage sales

These are excellent for buying accessories and unusual smalls. They are not usually that good for furniture, but you can never tell. I once bought at a garage sale a very nice Duncan Phyfe table that I was able to sell for a decent profit.

Since garage sales are part of our neighborhood landscape, I won't spend too much time on them.

Just remember:
1. Carry cash in small bills, as most people won't take checks, unlike an auction house.
2. Go early. Prices being lower than elsewhere, sales are usually brisk.
3. Make lower offers than you'd expect to pay. Garage sales are organized to raise cash without thought of the value of the products. This gives you the opportunity to buy cheap. Did I hear you say great?
4. Many big garage sales are advertised in the Friday paper. Make a list of them and mark their addresses on a spare map so that you can visit as many as possible in as short a time as possible.
5. Don't dawdle talking to people. Remember that you don't want to buy junk and you certainly want to avoid the table with the broken leg that you can easily repair, even though it's so cheap. It's not worth the trouble. You have far more important things to do with your time.

Enough on garage sales, other than one more tip. If you have to visit a large number of them, send your spouse or partner to look at some of them instead of both of you arguing and falling over each other. Why don't you split up and cover twice the number of sales in the same time?

Buying from other dealers

This is an excellent source for products, but only if you apply those smarts that we know you have. After all, why hasn't the dealer already sold it to a regular customer?

When I first got involved in the antique business I was surprised at how much trading went on between dealers. It didn't make sense to me that about forty percent of the turnover was done within the industry itself. After a while I realized that there were two main reasons for this. The first was that the business is full of amateurs playing at it. Most of these dealers enter the business for the camaraderie and for something to do, rather than to make money. That's okay, if you prefer it that way. I however, do not recommend it. The reason? Most lose money.

The second reason why so much trading is done among dealers is that it's so much easier to buy that way. After all, if you don't have the profit motive driving you (as you and I do!) why should you go out into that dark night, drive fourteen miles to the auction, and possibly come home without buying anything? It's much easier to buy that discounted vase in the nearby mall.

"What's wrong with that?"

Nothing, except that half your customers may have already seen it there and remembered its price. Always keep in the forefront that you are the best in the business. Your customers keep coming back to you because you have a constant supply of new, unusual items. They expect it from you.

I want to illustrate this point. It's important.

I have a wonderful old lady as a regular customer. I'll call her Mildred. Since Mildred is retired and of sufficient disposable income, she pampers herself by spending one thousand dollars on herself every month. She has excellent taste, likes the unusual, and is a knowledgeable shopper. At her age and standing, she expects personal service and unique products. She buys them mainly from me and not in the antique mall where she goes to have coffee and a wonderful cheesecake every week. If she so much as saw a product in my shop that I bought in that mall, I would lose a very nice sale every month.

What is the lesson here?

Act like the professional businessman that you are. Don't buy from other dealers unless it's an absolute bargain, and certainly not from nearby dealers. Do put in the hours to buy new products, even if you have to drive fourteen miles in pouring rain.

If you want to buy from other dealers, go out of town to do it. It's critical to your financial well-being.

Buying from newspaper advertisements

This is a good way of buying, but like all things, there's a downside.

The downside is that you could drive clear across town to buy that beautiful antique wardrobe, a collector's piece, only to find that it's a broken-down has-been and not worth fifty bucks!

When buying from newspaper adverts, follow one golden rule: Ask, ask, and ask again for details on the phone before you go out. Be specific. Make a list before you call. Ask about the hinges, if there are any cracks, if the mirrors are perfect, how about the hardware? Is it all there? etc.

If you feel that's rude, just remember that it's a lot cheaper, and certainly less disappointing than spending twenty bucks on gas in the heat of the day, only to come away empty-handed and mad at the jerk advertising it in such glowing terms!

What have we learned about buying from newspaper adverts then?

Make yourself a list of questions.

Ask for details.

Be specific and very pointed so that any hesitancy gives you a clue that all is not as it should be. Ask the price up front.

And when you go out to buy it?

Follow the golden rules. Would you like it in your own house? Is it old? unusual? so on, and so on, and so on!

In concluding this section on newspapers, I must tell you about two excellent publications that I highly recommend. Both are specialist antique papers and are full of valuable information. They will certainly help you to keep up-to-date with all the industry trends, such a necessary factor for the professional dealer. A useful feature of the *Antique Traveller*, published in Mineola, Texas, is the National Antique Show Calendar. It's a must for the serious dealer. *The Antique Almanac,* printed in Bowie, Texas, concentrates on rural towns actively developing their antique trade. It covers their progress by relating very interesting anecdotes. Both are excellent reading. Subscribe to them.

Buying from private sellers

"Why this section? Surely it's the same as buying from newspaper advertisements?"

Not quite. It can be easier, particularly when buying smalls. The same rules apply, but often you can arrange for the private seller to bring the product to you. It saves a lot of hassle.

"How can you get sellers to offer you their family antiques?"

Easy. Get yourself a small yellow pages ad on your business. Put in it that you buy and sell unusual, good quality antiques and the phone will ring constantly.

Most booth holders never even think of this.

"Why is that?"

Because they only have a booth and think that they are too small. Nonsense, is what I say. All you need to do is have the phone installed at home and on the yellow pages ad you can put the mall address.

"But that's another overhead!"

Yes, but well worth it. Not only will you draw customers to your booth, but you will also have sellers offering you product before it gets on the market. The savings from buying this way will more than cover your costs and give you a steady stream of merchandise to choose from. My friend Beverly just bought a whole bunch of very nice ashtrays this way. If I had been offered them, I would have bought them myself.

All right. To summarize:

1. Ask, ask, and ask again! Pointed questions will ensure that you are not going to drive twenty miles to look at a lemon.

2. Get yourself a yellow pages advertisement to ensure a steady stream of new merchandise at reasonable prices.

Go get 'em. With so much merchandise available, you can start being picky. Nice position to be in, isn't it?

Antique shows

I don't go to many unless I'm just going to browse. Dealers pay a lot of money just to get a temporary booth at these and as a result, real bargains are few and far between. I always think that antique shows are really designed for wealthy people. Certainly not for a pack rat, bargain hunter like me. There are always exceptions of course. Maybe you will have better luck than I have, but don't hold your breath! Flea markets are a much better bet.

Importing your own products

Not for you at this stage. When you get your co-op set up and are selling volumes, it will be worth thinking about. I do my own importing. Since it's such a huge and complex procedure, I am writing a book called *Budget Buying European Antiques* to cover this subject. At this stage, forget it. Later on it will be well worthwhile.

Flea markets in the USA; car boot sales in the UK

This is a very popular way of buying antiques, particularly in summer. In many parts of the country, flea markets are a weekly feature throughout the year. In Texas, the one in Southlake on Highway 114 has grown year by year, and in Wales I always buy at the ever-enlarging Stormy Down on the M48.

Flea markets are so popular with antique dealers because they offer a wide variety of merchandise at reasonable prices. Since they are held weekly, you can restock in small increments and conserve cash when times are tough.

"So what should I do at flea markets?"

Flea markets in the U.S.A.; Car boot sales in England.

The question should be, "What should I *not* do at flea markets?"

You should not buy the first products that interest you. You should cover the whole market first and then come back to the ones that caught your attention. Just so you remember where and what they were, you should draw a sketch and mark in the product and location of anything that interested you on the first pass.

"Is there any special technique in negotiating with flea market dealers?"

Sure there is. It is one that I use to great effect and it saves me a lot of money. I learned it from my terrific Arab friends in the bazaars of Saudi Arabia and Kenya. It goes like this:

During my preliminary walk-around, I never indicate to the dealer what I am interested in. If I want to check a piece for quality, I do so after picking up a few other pieces that I don't have the slightest interest in. If you watch the dealer closely while you are doing this, you will see his mind register the first product that you examined as the one that you really want, particularly if you make a big show of it. Did I hear you say that I'm cheating? Never! I'm just being smart like you are.

What usually happens while I'm doing this is that he will disclose his initial asking price. Ignore all the figures he gives you, except that of the piece you really want. Then walk away.

"Walk away?"

Yes. Walk away.

Ten minutes later I'm back. Again I pick up the first item that I examined so thoroughly and ask the dealer if he will take a lower price for it. Almost certainly, he will. Furrowing my brow, I hesitate … and then put it down again. Now I pick up the piece that I'm really interested in, and ask its price again. I will almost guarantee that now the dealer will give you a lower price than he originally gave you on your first go-around. Again I hesitate, then I execute the coup de grace.

I ask if he will give me a discount on the two of them and what the price will be on each piece. You can bet your bottom dollar that he will lower his price on both of them!

I then purchase only the item I want at the final discounted figure.

"What a long rigmarole," I can hear some skeptics saying.

Then there are those who are just trying to make this month's rent.

Sure it is. But after buying ten items, the savings are substantial.

The point here is that every little bit is money in the bank. If you get into the habit of purchasing at the very best possible price all the time, even if it takes some effort, then you are a true professional.

Talking of professional, if you buy a lot at flea markets, get yourself a fold-up cart. One of those with the large wheels and the metal frame basket. You will love them to death when you have six pieces to carry to your car that is parked about one mile away. Why is it that one of those pieces is always an ornate occasional table or antique hat rack?

"What kind of products do most dealers look for at flea markets?"

Almost always smalls, not furniture. The exception is small tables or chairs. The difficulty I always have with flea markets is that I have to stretch my imagination to the limit to picture what that rusty, ornate gate will look like in my flower filled, thickly carpeted store. My friend Beverly, on the other hand, is an expert at this. She can see beauty when all I can see is junk, and she is usually right. If you can do this, you have a great talent. She once bought some rusty old iron gates. When I saw them I said "Shuuuuure!" She just laughed. She laughed even louder when all four sold within three weeks and I had to ship one to Macon, Georgia.

But the one item that really surprised me was the urinal. Yes, you heard right. She bought a urinal. Not just an ordinary urinal, you understand, but a lovely amber glass one with a long spout. Those of you who are my age will remember using them if you ever had an extended stay in the hospital in the 1950s. Beverly sold it as an unusual "what-not." The buyer, a lady in her twenties, loved the unusual "what-not's" shape and I'm sure still hasn't figured out what it was originally for. She probably puts flowers in it.

The big feature of flea markets for antique dealers is the variety, which is certainly better than at most auctions. Look for lamps, pictures, porcelain, crystal and cut glass, old iron-work clocks, and wooden boxes.

But come early. All the best items are usually snapped up by the early birds. Some eager ones even come with flashlights while it's still dark. Also remember that there are professional flea marketeers who give themselves away with their organized setups, and then there are those that are just trying to make this month's rent. Which are you going to buy from? Smart, very smart!

How about a story then? It's about a professional flea marketeer. I had heard about this lady from Beverly, who often bought from her. One thing I must say up front is that her products are always first class, but her technique is even better!

Every Tuesday, many of the expert dealers turn up at the Southlake flea market at the crack of dawn. That's when most serious dealers are already buying. Not this lady, no sir! She sets up every Tuesday at 9 a.m. sharp—banker's hours! By this time, all the buyers are waiting for her in one huge crowd instead of dribbling in one at a time. Even before she unloads, they are taking things out and trying to beat each other to her best products. It's like a shark feeding frenzy! To see normally cold, logical dealers almost fighting to grab an item surprised me when I first saw it.

You know what her purpose is, don't you?

Well … when she quotes her highest price for that item the dealer is clutching in his grubby hand, all he can do is to pay. All the other dealers are staring at him and he doesn't want to look foolish in front of them, particularly as he has almost been in a fight just to get hold of it.

She always gets top prices. Smart, very smart!

Chapter 5 review

This chapter has a lot of information compressed into its pages. As usual, I will recap so that when you are in a hurry you can get the main points.

1. **If you want it for your home, buy it**. Remember that guideline when looking at merchandise.

2. **Your sources for merchandise are auctions, estate sales, garage sales, antique shows, flea markets, and sales from newspapers**. Mark the addresses on your information bulletin board. When going to garage sales, mark their locations on a map so that you have a planned route. Get rid of your spouse or partner for a morning by sending him or her to other sales.

3. **Buying from dealers: Never buy from dealers in your own backyard**. It will cost you customers.

4. **Newspaper sales: Ask, ask, and ask some more**. Save yourself a long, hot journey for nothing. You can see lemons closer to home.

5. **Private sales: Yellow pages advertisement is a must**.

6. **Flea markets: Don't buy until you've done a go-around**. Use a bargaining technique. Go early. Please, please, don't get caught in a feeding frenzy! Otherwise, flea markets are the best place to buy. If you are careful you can get top quality products. If not, you will become a junk dealer! Shame on you then.

$$\$ \ \$ \ \$ \ \$$$

What a long chapter. Now you know where to get the antiques to fill your booth, or booths, and you are truly on your way to success. But how do you cost your merchandise and how much should you charge? Read on.

6. Buying Merchandise

Are you excited about your new business? Do you feel your confidence rising with your increasing knowledge?

Congratulations! Take time out to pat yourself on the back, you deserve it. Not only have you learned a lot from what we covered in the previous chapters, but I bet that you have also picked up a few tips of your own.

That's what's so exciting about the antique business—it's still growing and no one has cornered the market on knowledge.

So far we have covered getting started, the definition of antiques, judging your customer base, and where and how to find merchandise. Now we have to decide whether we are going to buy all this merchandise in a professional manner or just chance it, like most antique dealers do. If you think I'm wrong, just ask a few dealers in your mall to tell you how they decide on what price to pay for an antique chair, for example.

I guarantee that ninety percent will say, "Oh, I'm experienced. I know what I can sell it for, and so I buy it at half that price."

Wrong!

If they only knew how wrong they were, they would feel extremely foolish.

For a start, all chairs are not equal. A Chippendale design is completely different from a Regency style. Some are a better

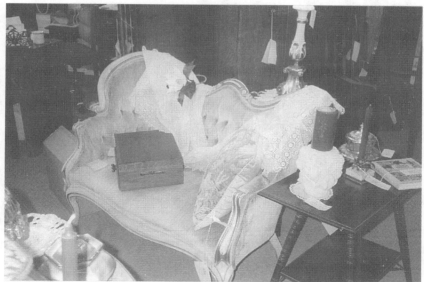

All chairs are not equal.

quality, some prettier, and some are more sought after.

More important than that, some dealers have no idea what their overhead is and certainly do not consider this factor in either their buying or selling price. Taking the easy way out, they lump all expenses into their one hundred percent mark-up, and then wonder why they made no profit at the end of the year.

"Why do they do that?"

Because they don't want to bother with doing their home-work. **They ignore all over-**

A Chippendale design is completely differ-ent from a Regency design.

head in the hope that doubling the price will cover expenses and make them a profit. This is a major failing of most dealers and accounts for why there are far too few successful ones.

How can you sensibly add up all your expenses—gas, rent, your time, wear and tear on your vehicle, theft, and breakage— and still give a hefty discount to the buyer on the already heavily discounted price shown on your price tag?

Of course you can't. Not unless you have calculated everything in, bought at the right price, and marked up sufficiently.

"How do I do this without being the high-powered Harvard honors graduate mentioned in your first chapter, which you promised I wouldn't have to be in order to be successful in the antique business?"

Very simply. You spend an hour working out a "ready-reckoner" rule-of-thumb system.

Systems, systems, systems! They are the key to success!

I will give you mine, but remember that nothing is set in concrete. Take what applies to you, throw away what doesn't, and modify it to suit yourself. Then use it, use it, and use it again when buying and selling.

Here's what you should do to start:

1. Set a realistic sales target for the year. We will use $20,000. This is a fair start for a single booth operation.

2. Set a realistic net profit that you expect to earn. (We will use 20% as our figure for this example. Don't forget it's net, not gross.) Therefore, our profit is $4000.

3. Add up your estimated overhead for one year; pro rata the long-term items.

   Example:

Booth rent @ $250 per month ($250 x 12)	= $3,000
Your pay for 20 hours work per month (20 x $10 x 12)	= $2,400
Gas usage @ $40 per month	= $480
Insurance @ $60 per month	= $720
Wear and tear on vehicle/booth repairs	= $560
Breakages and theft @ $20 per month	= $240
Total	= $7,400

4. Add the profit and overhead and subtract this from your gross sales.

5. The result will be the total buying budget for the whole year.

6. To obtain your pricing formula to ensure your desired 20% net profit on gross sales, divide 100 by your annual purchasing budget and multiply it by your total sales target for the year. The figure of 100 is an estimated price of pieces you will buy in the first year. Watch it and modify your calculations as you progress through the year.

Now I know that real accountants will poke all sorts of holes through this. Frankly, I don't care, and neither should you. All you are doing is giving yourself a safe basis figure to start with. I call it the multiple factor. Once you have been trading for some time you will have to modify your multiple factor, but by then you will have concrete figures to go on instead of estimated ones.

7. This multiple factor is the factor by which you must multiply the cost of each piece of inventory purchased in order to obtain your sales price and reach the 20% desired net profit on your gross sales.

Example:

1. Target gross sales figure	$20,000
2. 20% expected net profit	$4,000
3. Overhead (see calculation)	$7,400
4/5. Buying budget [$20,000 - $11,400 (#2 plus #3)]	$8,600

6. 100 ÷ 8,600 x 20,000 = 232, i.e. 2.3 is your multiple factor.

Therefore, if you buy a $100 item you will have to sell it at $232. If you intend to give discounts as sales incentives you should build this up. I would suggest that you round your factor out to 2.5, making your necessary sales price $250. This gives you $18 or 7.75 percent as a safety factor for discounts or other costs. Many good dealers use a multiple factor of 3. I do, but it can only be done on really unusual and good antiques.

Now picture this: You walk into an auction and see a beautiful draw-leaf table. You have just sold one in your booth for $400.

You take out your calculator, divide $400 by 2.5 and you now know your buying limit is $160.

Easy, isn't it?

Once you have this fixed in your head, life becomes so much easier. Not only that, you can sleep better knowing that you are well in control and know what you are doing. Doesn't that feel good?

How about when a flea market dealer sticks on $30 for that porcelain vase? He simply won't go down! Using your trusty calculator all you have to decide is, "Can I sell it at $75?" If the answer is yes, then part with your money.

Now you have a ready-reckoner to guide you in buying and selling. Obviously my system is only a guide. You will have different circumstances and different costs. The point is, you now have a reasonably calculated basis to start with and not just a hope that by doubling your purchase price, your overhead and profit are taken care of.

I know you're smart. Modify it to suit yourself, but don't, I repeat don't, ignore it. If you base your purchasing and selling on facts, you can't go far wrong. Too many people have lost money in this business because they work only on instinct and not on facts. Please don't be one of them.

One more thing. Do not cut out the figure for your own pay and say, "I'll make it in the profit." You must calculate your own time in. After all, you wouldn't work free for someone else, would you?

My wife is an accountant. She gets exasperated with me for always using my ready-reckoner calculation, but even she has to admit that it works for me. Sometimes we do our own separate calculations, she in a professional way, and me using my amateur method. It's surprising how close I am. Close enough for me anyway.

Price points

Most dealers think about price points when selling, few think about them when buying.

So what is a price point?

It's a price below which you want to be, but it's also more than that. I always think of price points as points of resistance. When selling, go above them and psychologically the customer thinks of twice the price. Stay one cent below, and the customer thinks they are getting a great bargain. One builds resistance against the sale, and the other builds momentum for it.

Here are the recognized retail price points: 10, 15, 20, 25, 50, 100, 500, 1000, and 5000 dollars. Stay one cent below these and customers think of the first digit only. Go above, and they think of the next whole number.

You don't believe me?

Try it. What number do you think of if I say $9.95? Nine of course, not ten. The reason is that the brain registers the first number and because it's a pleasant thought, you take the easy way out. "It's under ten dollars," you think, not, "Heck, it's actually ten!"

Okay, but that's for selling. How about when buying?

Buying price points obviously affect the selling price. Bear this in mind and fight, fight, and fight some more, for the lower figure.

Example:

A dealer wants $165 for a table.

Insist on $149.95. Tell him you'll pay cash. I know it's only $15 but look how much better it is when you are selling the same item.

$165 x 2.5 = $412

$149.95 x 2.5 = $375

Since the first digit is the one that registers in the customer's mind, they kid themselves that it's almost $100 cheaper. It isn't, but all that registers is the 3 and the 4 digit numbers.

Never, never, forget to take the price point into consideration when purchasing. A little more effort in negotiating will reap you great rewards. All it takes is a conscientious effort on your part.

I hope that you become good at using these techniques. People might even think that you have some African and Arab influences in your life, just like me. I am very proud to be called a friend of the descendants of some of history's most famous traders. Don't forget that it was the folks in the Arabian peninsula and the Indian subcontinent who were the first traveling merchants. If you've ever bargained with an Indian trader in the Mombasa, Kenya, bazaar, you will realize what masters they are. They can get you to pay double and still feel good about yourself. Now that's an expert's technique. On the other hand, I learned something that gave *me* the edge.

In many eastern religions, Friday is considered a special day and devout practitioners always go to the mosque on Friday evenings. The reason is that they work on an Islamic calendar where Friday is our Sunday. Over time, Asian traders have developed a superstitious feeling about the first customer to come into their store on a Friday morning. They simply must not let the customer leave without him or her buying something. It sets the tone for the whole day and the following week. A sale to Friday's first customer means that the coming week's sales will be good and vice versa.

Guess what day I used to go shopping in Nairobi's bazaar?

Boy, did I get some great bargains!

Have fun. Use your head and apply price point techniques to buying and selling merchandise.

Bidding techniques

This usually applies to auctions and estate sales. Since you already know how to work out your decision buying price, I won't say too much more. I will, however, take a few moments of your time to go over some useful techniques.

Remember the one about entering into the bidding as the tempo slows? Do you remember why?

It's because you want your opposition to run out of adrenaline (steam) before you do, so that they lose heart and stop bidding against you earlier.

Here's another useful tip: If the price is still considerably below the figure you are prepared to pay, jump the figure up substantially instead of going up in small increments.

Example:

Three of you are bidding on a lovely French oak wardrobe. Your decision buying price is $1,200 but the bidding is only at $800. You came in as the back-and-forth had slowed, so you know that the other two buyers are already at limits. The auctioneer looks at you. In a loud—note loud—clear voice, you call "one thousand dollars!" The immediate effect is that one buyer, if not the two, will drop out because they are intimidated by your action, backed up by your loud decisive call.

Gang leaders in Los Angeles call this "juice." It means power, prestige, dominance, and a "don't mess with me" attitude all in one.

Of course, the other bidders may think that you are an idiot paying too much. However, since you did your homework earlier on, you know you aren't.

Smile smugly at them with that "I know something you don't" look and rub it in. The puzzled frown on their faces is reward enough for all those boring calculations that you had to do.

Fun isn't it?

Offers

A difficult one.

"Why?"

Because usually when you are making an offer on an item, it's face-to-face with the seller. That means embarrassment with a capital E, particularly if the seller is a little old lady with a downcast look.

Don't let that fool you. You're a professional, remember? Under no circumstances should you offer more than the low price you had in mind, and certainly not more than your decision buying price.

Here I would like to tell you a funny story. It might teach you that all is not what it seems to be.

My friend Beverly (yes, that Beverly, the one with the wonderful advice) had an old lady come in offering her some rugs. Bent over, her voice quivering, she told Beverly that they belonged to her mother and were very, very old. "At least fifty years old," she said. "I wouldn't sell them," she continued, "but I need the money to pay my rent."

Although she won't admit it to this day, Beverly, being the kindhearted person that she is, bought them for $75 each. As I understood it, she really felt good when the little old lady thanked her profusely as she left. Not only had she done her good deed for the day, but she had also bought some bargains.

Now I must admit that the rugs weren't that bad. But old? Never!

Two days later, that little old lady was in my shop selling me her "mother's old lace." I could swear that she had tears in her eyes. In normal circumstances I would have bought the tablecloths, but my bank balance was down and I was sweating on the rent due three days later. Feeling sorry for her, I escorted her to the door and watched her bent figure shuffle out. I felt like a real dog!

That was until I saw her straighten up, open the trunk of a brand new top-of-the-line Oldsmobile, and throw her "mother's old lace" on top of a pile of other new merchandise.

Such is the antique business. Watch out for little old ladies bearing bargains!

Now you know why I keep hammering that professional attitude bit.

When making offers, hang tough, and stay focused. It will save you lots of money and keep egg off your face. I know, I've wiped a lot off mine.

Co-op buying

Co-op buying, sometimes called volume buying, is not for everyone. For a start, most antique dealers are an independent lot. The very nature of the business breeds individuality, as do the products.

So what is co-op buying? And how can you get it to work for you?

Well, the first thing you have to do is to get together with other dealers to buy in bulk. If you can coordinate this, you can all save a bundle.

How do you do this?

By putting up a notice on your mall bulletin board and getting a group of you together to approach a wholesaler. Propose that you buy a number of pieces from him if he gives your co-op a bulk discount. After all, he gives such discounts to restaurants and bed and breakfasts buying more than one piece. You might even ask him to throw in free delivery to your mall, since your group will be spending a lot of money with him. Buying this way saves you money, and solves the main problem of your individual tastes at the same time. Since a wholesaler will have a warehouse full of merchandise, each of you can select the pieces you individually need. Obviously you can't do it at auctions or estate sales, but you can certainly do it when buying from wholesalers.

As I said, it's not for everyone. It requires organization, extra work, and the ability to cope with a bunch of mavericks! If you try it, I guarantee that you will be stuck with the organizing. Think about it long and hard. The rewards are great, but so is the responsibility.

Cash is king!

We all know this one don't we?
Use it to get the best possible price. There's nothing better.

Recently I was on a buying trip to Wales. In the Pumping Station in Cardiff, the Welsh capital, I saw a beautiful French country cabinet. The lady was using it to great effect in displaying her Flow Blue plates. Noticing how many people stopped to admire it, I inquired if she wanted to sell it. She adamantly refused. Nothing would make her budge. "No way!" she said. Some ten minutes later I mentioned my interest to a nearby dealer. He told me that he had also been after that fine piece for many months and had received the same response.

In our discussion, he mentioned that he had even offered her £700, payable in two installments. This gave me a clue.

Waiting till close of business on what had obviously been a slow day, I went back and spread £800 in notes on her table. I told her that I had fallen in love with the unit and she could either put the money into her pocket without issuing me a receipt, or she could push it back to me. She hesitated, looked at the bills, and then scooped them up.

It looked terrific in my store in Grapevine.

Cash can be used for more than just getting the best price, can't it?

Consignment

Use consignment techniques sparingly and they can earn you profit without cash outlay. Too many consignment pieces, however, become an administrative nightmare and can cause legal and other problems.

In the next chapter on pricing merchandise, I discuss marking up the price sufficiently to give a discount as a persuasive sales tool. Since consignment pieces are other people's property, your freedom of action to use discounts is severely limited. It is also surprising how consignors resent the amount of discount you gave, once their property is sold, even if you discussed it in detail before and had their approval. The human animal is the strangest one on God's earth.

Don't accept consignments except very sparingly, and only with exceptional pieces.

Who pays for breakages and theft, disappointment at lower prices, and bad feelings if it doesn't sell—all make for a bad scene. Used sparingly, consignments make sense. Just make sure that you write down the conditions on which you put them into your booth and get the consignor to sign the agreement.

ntifying quality

vVhat is this intangible thing called quality?

Perfect condition, nothing broken, no blemishes, good hardware, no chips, no cracks or stains, no broken handles, etc.

Yes. All of the above. But also appearance.

Is it different, pretty, striking, unusual, and would you have it in your own home? If yes, you have a piece of great quality.

Price doesn't really enter into it. Price follows quality and not the other way around.

After a while it becomes very easy to spot quality. It usually costs money!

Seriously now, I bet you are already capable of spotting quality and are getting better at it daily. Never stop learning is the best advice that I can give you here.

Buying reproductions

Ugh!

Works for some. Many dealers do this, and some even make a little money at it, although I don't know how.

The question is, should YOU buy and sell reproductions? Not if you want to gain a reputation as a professional antique dealer and make money at it.

Remember what I told you?

So much reproduction antique-type furniture is pouring into the U.S., Canada, and Europe, that the prices are dropping dramatically. As I mentioned, those mahogany credenzas that used to sell for $800 are now available for as little as $350. You can bet your bottom dollar that someone is losing money. I did. Please don't let it be you.

You want to know how I, as a so-called expert, lost money on reproductions? I'll tell you reluctantly. After all, none of us likes to feel a fool, do we? This is what happened:

On a recent buying trip in England, I bought a large number of pieces of furniture at my favorite wholesaler. I enjoy my visits and the dealer and I were having fun. I was buying … he was counting up the money he was making! Come to think of it, he was getting the better deal. No wonder he was so jolly!

We were both loose, kidding around, and this made me forget about taking care of business. In the back of the warehouse I spotted a very pretty French curio cabinet, and without giving it my usual thorough inspection, I bought it. In fairness to the dealer, it had only just come in and he also was not aware that it was a reproduction.

Once I had it in my shop, I realized that it was a repro, but based on my multiple factor I had to sell it at $2,200. No way, Jose! Still … I tried.

I bet you can guess what happened next.

A young lady came up to me one day and asked me sweetly, "What is so special about that curio cabinet? I have seen the same cabinet down the road at $875 and also in the next town at $800." Her eyes said it all.

Three days later I saw two more of them in an antique auction in Fort Worth. They were listed as French antique curio cabinets!

I sold it fast at $700 and lost money.

I never did that again. Even an old gray-beard like me is entitled to make one mistake. Learn from mine and it will save you a bundle. Have you ever heard the saying, "If I make a mistake it's your fault, but if I do it again it's my fault?" Now that I've told you about my own boo-boo, you won't do it yourself will you?

But here's the real problem: How do you tell a reproduction when buying antiques?

Check the hinges, screws, glue, inside finish, and unevenness of the decorative carving. Antiques have old rusty hinges, off-set screw slots, cracked glue, rough, dirty inside finishes, and uneven carved decorations.

Reproductions have new hinges, new screws, tough glue, clean inside finish, and machine-made, even decorative carving.

Don't think that antique auctions only sell antiques. Far from it! At a recent auction, I was surprised to see that almost eighty percent of the furniture offered was reproduction.

How else can you identify a reproduction at an auction?

They never call each piece an antique. They call it an *antique style* Victorian settee. Read the descriptions carefully and you will soon pick it up. If it doesn't say positively and categorically antique, it isn't one.

"Can I get my money back if I buy it under misrepresentation?"

You can, but believe me, it's not worth the effort. All those disclaimers on the walls and on all the paperwork make it almost impossible, even if you had a million dollars. I'm sure you've seen them yourself.

"All goods are sold as is and are not vouched for," is the best one I've seen.

Avoid buying reproductions, but if you must, be warned. The public is not that gullible. You're too good at antiques to ruin your reputation.

Keeping cool

"What a strange section."

No! Not if you think about it.

What is the overriding factor to consider when buying? Use your loaf (as they say in England) or head, as they say in the good old U.S. of A!

That's right, use your head. Never buy with your heart. Whether you are buying at auctions or estate sales, are making an offer, or are using cash to buy low, never forget to stay cool and stick to your decision buying price. That's why keeping cool is the sign of a professional. Look for them, they're easy to spot.

Steely-eyed, they walk around or bid at auctions totally composed. You can almost see their minds working their ready-reckoner amounts as they juggle buying and selling figures mentally or on their calculators.

I never realized how much we stand out until a lady came up to me at a previewing.

"You seem to know what you are doing," she said, "will you please help me?"

I did, and it gave me the idea for this book. Thank you, the sharp-eyed lady at the previewing in Dallas. You had no idea what you started.

Look at yourself in the mirror. See those squinting eyes? I bet you are beginning to look like that. There aren't too many of us and it's a fairly exclusive club.

Welcome!

Chapter 6 review

1. **Establish yourself a multiple factor** for costing and buying.

2. **Use price points** when buying and selling. That will make you more price competitive.

3. **When bidding, come in late, decisively, and with "juice."** Use these techniques to the max and intimidate your competition.

4. **When making offers, hang tough**! Remember that little old lady selling me her mother's antique lace. "To pay my rent," she cried, wrenching at my heart. It was a different story when I saw her new Oldsmobile. I wish I could afford one myself.

5. **Co-op buying. Do it if you are an organizer.** You could save yourself a lot of money and make many new friends. Avoid it if you are independent and like to do your own thing.

6. **Cash is king!** No more need be said.

7. **Consignments—too much trouble**. Avoid taking in consignments except in small doses and only if they are exceptional pieces.

8. Finding quality. **Appearance! appearance! and appearance! defines quality**. Cost also.

9. Buying reproductions. **Don't do it if you want to be known as a reputable antique dealer** and not lose money. Also remember the Trade Descriptions Act and mark a reproduction as such—no ifs or buts!

10. **Keeping cool means using your head to buy and sell**.

$ $ $ $ $

Another long chapter taught you a lot, I hope. You are now more knowledgeable than about seventy percent of the dealers I know. Let's make it one hundred percent so that you become the tops.

You can, you know.

7. Pricing Merchandise

"But we covered this in the previous chapter."

Most of it, but not quite all. There are still a lot of tips that need their own explanation and because we did all the heavy work in the previous chapter, this should be fun.

Where do we start? First let's see what we've got:

1. We have our purchase price and know we bought right.
2. We know our multiple factor is 2.5.
3. We know we must fit in with a selling price-point to move the merchandise quickly.
4. We know the quality of our item … good, I hope!

Now what we must do is coldly calculate our sales price and introduce a flexibility factor.

"A flexibility factor, what's that?"

I knew you'd ask. Your interest in your new business is obvious and on top of that you have an inquiring mind.

In any case, I know I told you to be coldly logical, and being flexible sounds very wishy-washy but you can be coldly logical and flexible at the same time, as long as you have a valid, calculated reason for being so.

"What can that reason be?"

The reason being that you want to sell the item as fast as possible, while making as much money as possible. In other words, you want to apply all factors in pricing your merchandise. It means that having established your necessary selling price by use of the multiple factor, you have to adjust it up or down depending on the nearest price point, the quality of the item, and a built-in reserve for a discount incentive.

"Sounds complicated."

Not really. You are now far more experienced and can therefore judge the perceived value more accurately. Remember that term—perceived value. It is important in deciding whether you can increase the price of goods beyond your normal mark-up. The easiest way to teach you this is to use an example.

Let's start with a very unusual, pretty, and good quality buffet. It cost us $160.

The necessary asking price is therefore $400.

What is the nearest price point for us? $399 or $499?

First, it is very unusual and pretty. The quality is also great, as it's a golden oak color. The hardware is first class and definitely very old and different. Its perceived value is therefore high.

Now can you guess the flexibility factor?

Did you decide to price it at $499?

Well done!

By considering its unusual color and its first class quality, you can go up to $499 and use the discount incentive to move the product faster if you have to. If someone falls in love with it at first sight and you don't have to use your discount incentive to sell it, you will make an extra $100. Of course, if it had been just a fair unit, you would have had to mark it at $399.

"But if I mark it at $399, the discount incentive will cause me to make less than I should," I hear you say.

No it won't. Remember that we calculated our multiple factor in Chapter 5 as 2.3 and then rounded it out to 2.5.

So what is the flexibility factor?

It's the factor you use to adjust your marked price up or down when taking the optimum price point, quality, and overall appearance into consideration, in order to sell the unit at the best profit margin and as fast as possible.

Easy when you know how, isn't it? Just remember, the perceived value and flexibility factor work hand in hand.

Reserves and overhead

There is little more to say in this section. I have already covered it extensively in our previous discourse.

Why do I mention it then?

So that you rest easy. Having built your overhead into your multiple factor and your reserve into the rounding up of the multiple from 2.3 to 2.5, you can feel confident when negotiating with a customer and using the discount incentive to close a sale. Worries about whether or not you made a profit will not disturb your sales pitch.

Can you now see why I hammer the homework and systems so much? Once you have your price based on facts, you can be safely flexible.

That is a very satisfying thought.

Sleep easy!

Layaways

A necessary evil. Everybody does it. If done coldly and logically it works. If not, you will have a bucket full of trouble and maybe a bunch of legal problems as well. But you have to do it.

Most dealers think that the purpose of layaway is to increase sales and that is true. Customers who would otherwise not buy your beautiful armoire will do so on payment terms. Some customers will do nothing else, even if they have the money to pay cash. It makes them feel more in control and satisfies their sense of security if they hold on to the money and pay you over time.

"Is that the only purpose of a layaway policy?"

No, and that's the mistake that most dealers make.

The purpose of giving terms, in addition to enabling you to sell to customers short of cash, is to 1) develop a long-term customer relationship, and 2) allow you to make your full profit margin.

Surprised? Particularly at the second statement? I bet you are. Most amateur dealers don't even think of this. I will explain after we cover the first point.

By having a layaway program, you can continually sell to a customer setting up or changing out a home, but you must

She also wanted a pewter cross from Slovakia for her friend.

suggest this early in your relationship. Planting the seed is what I call it.

Here's how:

1. Inquire whether your customer is looking to add a piece to existing furniture or to completely redecorate. This plants the idea of the redecorating possibility.

2. Then suggest that she might like to add to the piece she has bought and point out that there is no limit to the number of items you would put on layaway for her.

I did this only yesterday. A lady had been looking at a very large ornate mirror in my shop for the past week. She also wanted a pewter cross from Slovakia for her friend. Since she was unable to pay for both at the same time, I offered to put them both on terms for a month so that she could save up a bit more. Gratefully she accepted. Not only did I sell two pieces, but I also made two people happy!

"The lady and her friend?"

No. The lady and me!

Try this technique. You will be surprised how many customers will consider changing the whole decor of a room, just by you suggesting layaway. Subtle but effective, it sells more than one piece.

Now to the second point—to allow you to make your full profit. Puzzled you, didn't it?

"What does profit have to do with layaway?" I hear you ask, "If anything, it eats into it!"

Yes, if you treat layaway as a normal sale, which it isn't. You'd be surprised how many dealers sell an item on payment terms and still give the discount as a sales incentive.

Don't do it.

Your overhead keeps piling up on the item until you get paid in full, and after two months your profit is eroded. Don't forget that you just might have sold that merchandise for the full price during the payment period and bought another piece that you might have, with luck, also sold.

It is best to have your layaway policy typed out on a sheet of paper, explaining that since there are administrative costs involved in operating the payment program, no discounts apply.

As a guide, here is a suggested one:

LAYAWAY PROGRAM

This layaway payment program is agreed to between _____
(hereafter known as the seller) and _____ (hereafter known as the
purchaser) on _____ 1996. It is made in good faith by both the seller and
purchaser in accordance with the following conditions.

1. The seller agrees to sell to the purchaser item _____ at a
   total price of _____, inclusive of all state, county, and federal taxes.

2. The title and ownership to the said above property will remain with the seller
   until the full payment detailed above is made in accordance with the conditions
   stipulated in this agreement.

3. On completion of the full and final payment, the title and ownership of the above
   detailed property shall be transferred to the purchaser by the seller, subject to the
   purchaser having finalized the full payment and complied with the conditions
   stipulated in this agreement. The seller agrees that if all payments and conditions
   are met, the seller will not unreasonably withhold the said title and transfer of
   ownership of the stipulated property.

4. The conditions of the layaway program are

   1. A 25 percent deposit of _____ is paid by the purchaser on signing of
      this agreement.

   2. The period of the layaway program is 60 days from date of signing.

   3. Three equal payments of _____ are to be made on _____ (date)
      and_____(date) and _____ (date).

   4. A late payment grace period of 2 days only will be allowed by the seller on
      each due date, unless a mutually agreed change is approved by both par-
      ties in writing.

   5. If purchaser does not comply with the above conditions, the detailed item
      will become the sole property of the seller with no recourse to its owner-
      ship by the purchaser. The seller can then dispose of the stipulated item
      with no further reference to the purchaser.

   6. The detailed item will remain in the possession of the seller until all pay-
      ments in item 3 are completed.

   7. Point of delivery is seller's designated property once full and final pay-
      ment is received.

   8. The seller is responsible for the good condition of the above detailed item
      while stored on seller's property.

   9. Due to the administrative costs involved in operating this layaway pro-
      gram, no discounts can be extended by the seller and the total price stipu-
      lated in item 1 of this agreement is the full and final price.

This document is signed by both parties without coercion and in a spirit of mutual
agreement.

Signed   Signed

_____   _____
Seller   Purchaser

Dated _____1996

The above is only a suggested agreement and you might want to add extra conditions to suit your particular circumstances.

The point here is that the total price, deposit, interim payments, and ownership is detailed. This makes sure that both parties understand their responsibilities.

Such a written agreement stood me in good stead when a lady bought a wardrobe from me, didn't make one interim payment, ignored my registered letters, and then came back one year later to demand her deposit back.

Finally, I would like to make two further points:

1. Once the agreement is signed, move the sold item into storage. It prevents damage and bad vibes if the customer happens to pop in.

2. Some dealers have a tear-off tag (see illustration). As each payment is made, they tear off a perforated section until only the heading section is left. If you prefer this system, ask around and someone will tell you where they get them locally. I prefer giving an official receipt for payments. It's more legal.

3. Keep a running journal in which you have all layaways detailed. Mark in every payment and run a reducing balance. If the customer asks for the balance, you are able to give it to them right away

A three section layaway ticket

instead of shuffling through paperwork. As it is, they are usually embarrassed as they have left their receipts behind and can't remember when they bought it. It saves face for both of you. It also makes you look very, very professional.

More important is that you can run down your journal and know whose payment is due or if anyone is overdue.

So remember, payment terms are good for sales. They build customer relationships and give you your full profit margin—but they need administrating.

"More work, right?"

I'm afraid so. But well worth it.

Discounts

Discounts are the most effective "big gun" in your sales arsenal. They can also kill you!

Giving discounts is the largest single factor in causing businesses to fail.

"Why?"

Because dealers use them as a panic measure to boost cash flow and not as a calculated sales tool. That won't happen to us though, because we built the discount factor into our multiple and even though we give discounts to close sales, they do not affect our desired and necessary profit margins in great measure.

But there's more. Since a discount is our most effective sales tool, we need to know how to use it to gain its maximum effect.

"So what do we do?"

For the first time I do not have a hard and fast rule. There seem to be so many ways of using discounts, that I shudder. Mainstream furniture stores use them en masse. You've seen the brightly colored fluorescent writing on their windows.

"Fifty percent off on all merchandise!" "No reasonable offer refused!" "Huge savings!" Many stores show listed prices and their discounted prices.

I have studied this phenomena and have concluded that there are two trains of thought:

1. By showing the huge discounts up front, the sellers appeal to the bargain hunter in all of us. It obviously works on some people. It turns others completely off.
2. Some sellers, on the other hand, believe that by advertising these discounts so openly, you build in a resistance. After all, they reason, who wants to be part of

the herd and what's wrong with the merchandise anyway? They're giving it away!

In the antique business, at least ninety-five percent of the
dealers believe in the first system. They have no idea why, but
everyone does it that way, so why shouldn't they?

I believe that it depends on what level of merchandise you are
selling.

I sell high-end antiques and the heavy discounting method has
never worked for me. In fact, when I tried it, it had a negative
effect. My well-to-do customers do not buy a product that they
think is anything but the best, and as such, they feel that
advertising a discount detracts from its value.

Please note I said *advertising* the discount. Even rich clients
want discounts, but they prefer them to be offered as a special
incentive due to them being special customers.

So here's my theory on the use of discounts: If you sell mid- to
low-quality antiques, advertise the discounts. It seems to work
for others, although I'm not really sure it actually does.

If you sell mid- to high-end antiques, don't even mention
discounts until negotiating the final sale. Then give them as a
special consideration for a very special customer.

My own pet hate is seeing price tags with three lowered prices
all crossed out. Who wants to think that they are buying an item
that no one else wanted and the dealer is off-loading? I'm not
cheap! And what's wrong with it anyway?

On the other hand, if one unusually low price is shown on the
tag, I might think that the dealer has made a mistake and I'll steal
it from under his nose before he realizes it!

Get the picture?

This chapter has been easier than I thought.

"Really? Why?"

Because we built in a discount factor at the beginning. If you
haven't, for goodness sake don't offer discounts. They will kill
you. One little comment here.

The increase in our multiple factor from 2.3 to 2.5 is not that
great. Playing with price points, discounts, and sales incentives
erodes it fast. That is why many knowledgeable dealers use a
multiple factor of 3. On the other hand, I have heard other dealers
say that they could never sell their merchandise marked up that
high. Make your own decision based on your own customer
income situation. How about 2.7?

The mirror was hers. Every time she looks at it she will remember us with a good feeling.

"Which discount technique should I use then?"

Try them both but watch the results very, very closely. If in doubt, only use discounts as a final sales tool to push the sale through. Don't forget, you don't sell antiques, customers buy them.

The very uniqueness of antiques guarantees that what one customer loves, the other hates. Once you see that dreamy look in their eyes, offer the discount as recognition of a very special customer. It's subtle and effective. They'll buy the item, and love you for it!

You don't believe me? The lady who bought the $900 mirror and the $180 crucifix does! Originally I had quoted $950 for the mirror and she was fully expecting to pay that much for it. Once she confirmed that she wanted to purchase it and was hesitating on the crucifix, I dropped the price to $900, but kept the crucifix at $180.

"Why not drop the price on the crucifix as well?"

Because the mirror was for her. Every time she looks at it she will remember us with a good feeling. The crucifix was a present for her friend. Out of sight, out of mind, right?

Taxes

Ugh!

Yes, none of us likes them.

In Chapter 9 I will cover these in more detail, but I have inserted this small section into "Pricing Merchandise" to highlight a mistake many of us make.

In considering the state of our business, many, if not most of us, subconsciously lump the taxes into our sales figures. Of course we know it's the government's and not our own money, but you'd be surprised how we all ignore this fact when our sales are marginal.

For your own good, ruthlessly deduct the tax from your daily and monthly sales when considering the overall health of your business. The 7.55% state sales tax in Texas and the higher Value Added Tax (VAT) of 17.5% in England make a huge difference.

Can you imagine that? 17.5%!

My deepest sympathy goes to all my English friends.

The other horrible fact to consider is that we have to actually pay the tax. If you're like most dealers, you will use it in your operating account, only to find that you don't have it when it's due.

Try not to do this. It's best to set up a separate account, but I'll cover that aspect in Chapter 9. Taxes give me the shivers, so let's move on to more pleasant matters.

Appraisers

Appraisers are expensive and I seldom use their services. That's not to say that you should ignore them totally. If you buy yourself the *Millers Antiques* and *Collins Encyclopedia* publications, you will have more than enough information to do your own appraisals, certainly on ninety-five percent of the merchandise that you will deal with on a day-to-day basis. Buy these books anyway, and on those quiet afternoons, go around the mall seeing if you can identify some of the better products in other booths.

Besides, you do want to look professional in front of your peers, don't you? What better way then to have them coming to you to borrow your *Collins Encyclopedia*!

The other use for these first rate reference books is to impress your customers. I had a brass lantern clock that I bought in England. *Millers* had a picture of an identical one in their antique clock section and I never failed to show this to customers inquiring about my clock. It made me look ever so professional!

It also sold the clock.

Having told you that your need of appraisers will be almost nonexistent, there is one situation where I use them. It has more to do with sales than their expertise, but you can always learn something new from them.

My friend Nancy is not just a highly knowledgeable and expert appraiser, she is also great fun to be with. When she and I get together, we feed off each other and both of us learns something new. Find yourself an appraiser like Nancy. It can be mutually beneficial and fun at the same time.

So when should you use an appraiser?

When you need a special sales incentive on a special antique piece or collection. Here is an example.

In 1993 I had the fortunate opportunity to buy a large number of smalls from Agatha Christie's housekeeper's son. Many of these were very unusual. To gain maximum sales impact, I had Nancy appraise the many pieces for me and I attached her valuation to each item in addition to my own. Although most of the people buying them had no idea who Nancy was, the attached appraiser's opinion enabled me to mark up the items slightly higher. The extra profit more than covered the cost of Nancy's fee, while also making me look very professional.

So! Make a friend of a local appraiser and have fun talking shop with him or her occasionally.

As I am writing this it amazes me how much longer these chapters become. Either there's more to everything than I thought, or else it really isn't such an easy business after all. That doesn't scare you anymore, does it?

Chapter 7 review

1. **The flexibility factor.** Use it to set a selling price based on quality and uniqueness. Go up or down to the nearest price point to make extra profits or to ensure that the item sells fast. Since we built our reserves and overhead into our multiple factor, we can sleep easy if we have to mark the item down to fit into the appropriate price point. Check it occasionally as expenses change.

2. **Layaways.** A necessary evil. Not only do they close a sale for you, but they should also be used to increase sales (remember the redecorating suggestion?), build long-term customer relationships, and ensure that you get your full profit margin. Write out an agreement, get

the customer to sign it, enter it into a journal, and check it to ensure payments are up-to-date.

3. **Discounts**! The most potent tool in your sales arsenal. Which method is best for you? Try both and make your own decision based on your customer income level. Remember that? We talked about judging your customer base in Chapter 4 when I said that it was the most important factor to consider in the antique business. If you've forgotten, go back and read it again! It will wind throughout your business forever.

4. **Taxes**. Take them out of your sales figure, deposit them elsewhere, and don't forget to pay them.

5. **Appraisers**. Make yourself a friend. It will be great fun shooting the breeze together. Not only that, but appraisals can be a wonderful sales tool when used in special circumstances.

$$\$ \ \$ \ \$ \ \$$

I hope you enjoyed reading this chapter as much as I enjoyed writing it.

We are now going to have fun, fun, and more fun! In the next chapter you are going to learn "mucho bene" about your own character and personality when we discuss setting up your own booth.

8. Setting Up Your Booth

This is going to be fun!

Setting up your booth so that it is interesting, attractive, and conducive to sales is of vital importance. Too many dealers simply position their furniture, add any and all accessories in a haphazard manner, and then wonder why customers avoid this mish-mash to spend time in the very attractive booth two aisles down.

Time and time again I walk into antique malls to be confronted either by sterile, parade-ground rows of antique furniture topped off with scattered afterthoughts, or a veritable junkyard shambles.

"But I don't know anything about decorating!"

Don't worry. You don't have to.

More important than talent is that you apply those smarts that I know you have. Do this in a coldly logical manner while injecting your bubbling, vivacious personality into your booth, and you'll do just fine.

You still look skeptical. Well, don't be. If I can do it, so can you. Trust me!

- First ... we shall **think** about decorating our booth. That's more than most dealers do.
- Second ... we shall use color, lights, mirrors, flowers, and a host of other accessories to **project an atmosphere**.

- Third ... we shall coordinate the items with which we are decorating to **replicate a room setting**.
- Fourth ... we shall change this out every time we sell a piece of furniture, or every three to four weeks to ensure that we **maintain customer interest**.
- Fifth ... we shall **give it ambiance** by the sparing use of potpourri oil.

"That's all very well, but I just don't have the feel or ability to tie it all together."

Did you think that I would desert you in your hour of need? Of course not. Here's the secret: Go buy yourself all those decorating magazines and steal their ideas. Those Victorian ones are particularly good. Note how they position lamps, pictures, and mirrors to get an effect. Observe, for example, how they place a lamp below and to one side of a mirror to reflect the light in beautiful patterns and note how they drape things to break up hard lines. Don't forget that your primary buyer is female. My apologies to the men, but it is true.

We shall use color, lights, mirrors, flowers, and a host of other accessories to "project an atmosphere."

Maximum visual impact! That's what we are trying to achieve.

Voila! (French for "there you go," for those who don't know.) You are an instant interior decorator. Now experiment by injecting your own personality and you are a very good interior decorator.

See what we have?

We have ourselves a plan to use all the decorating tools at our disposal to trap that unsuspecting customer and hold him or her as long as possible in our booth. Yes indeed! And we have the expert help of the highly paid magazine decorators to show us what to do. All that is left is to observe what techniques they use. There's no mystery to it, just the use of the power of observation that the good ol' Lord gave us all.

"So what decorating tools do we have?"

Color, flowers, mirrors, lamps, potpourri, lace, rugs, pictures, accessories, spotlights, pillows, and wrought-iron work—the list is endless. We have so much to work with to **create maximum visual impact!**

Add pretty, antique, quality furniture and watch out! Customers will be drawn to your booth like bees to honey!

Booth position

Get the one in the best trafficked area. That means the one in the front of the aisle at the entrance, if possible. A corner unit is also highly desirable because it is always visually interesting. Make sure that it has wall space with pegboard covering for hanging things. That goes for all booths. Insist on the pegboard, or on being able to put it up yourself. Many mall owners nowadays only give you a four-foot-high board to save costs, but since you are paying for all the space, insist on using it all. Dozens of holes to fill up on concrete or plasterboard walls are a pain in the proverbial rear when you leave, and in any case, they look unsightly. Without the pegboard you will be severely restricted in moving hanging items about. Insist that it be at least eight feet high, not just waist high. You want to use every inch of space possible and not pay for dead space.

Here's a tip:

As you are walking down the aisle, note which booth is most visible. That's the one you want. If it's occupied, put your name down for it in case it comes up in the near future. As a second choice, look for a corner one, and as a third, for the one slightly back from the bathrooms. You would be surprised how many people hang about outside bathrooms. (I mean husbands, wives, and children silly!)

Color coordination

Never use white. It's bland, totally unexciting, and clinically off-putting. The current in color is British racing green. When contrasted with cream, it looks very dignified. Try to stick to earth tones. Browns, maroons, peach, all the greens, old rose, and burgundy are good, as are all muted colors. Avoid bright garish yellows, bright reds, and fluorescent blues. Contrast two colors and it adds interest.

A quick story here.

Yesterday I went out to a house because the lady wanted to furnish it with antiques. It was a huge one, all brick and high ceilings. The owner didn't have the slightest idea of what to do. Stepping into the hall, I was dazzled by the tall white walls. They were so overpowering, that I almost put my sunglasses back on. This got me thinking. Why do developers always use white? The answer, of course, is that white is totally nondescript. It doesn't offend. At the same time, it has no personality and therefore it's a safe color. How about my thought for the day? Safe it might be, but it's also bland, and that's something none of us want, right?

Here's a secret: Go to your local paint store and talk to their in-house decorator. It's free. They also have color samples that you can take to your booth to check the effect of the interior lighting. Pick their brains, ask them about any interesting projects they're involved in, then go see them. Copy, copy, copy ... then add your own flair and personality.

One other tip: Don't just paint the walls flat. Use a newspaper, crumple it up, dip it in paint and dab it on. It makes a great speckled effect. *Faux pas*, some of the interior decorators call it, I think. The word means big or social mistake in French, but when done properly it gives a great effect. Where else but in the antique business can you make a "big mistake" and have it still look great?

Flowers

This is the best kept secret in the antique business. Hardly any booths or stores have them. Spend the money—get two or three arrangements and some vines from your local wholesaler. Sell them, and use them to add color, interest, and ambiance. It's

Flowers—the best kept secret in the antique business.

A terrific wrought-iron cross from Lourdes, France. I wanted to keep it for my own home.

cheaper than you think and makes you stand out. After all, don't all homes have indoor florals? Of course, they do. Remember, you are duplicating a room setting in your booth.

Drape the vines over mirrors, the corner of a wardrobe, or around that wall-hanging crucifix. I'll bet you that customers will buy them as a profitable add-on.

A few days ago I sold a terrific wrought-iron cross from Lourdes, France, to a delightful old lady. The vine I had draped around the stem made it an interior wall decorating piece instead of just an exterior item, and as such, I was able to increase the price. It was so neat looking that I was reluctant to sell it and wanted to keep it for my own home. Money changed my mind!

In closing this section, I must tell you about my flowers. When I first opened my shop, a very talented lady supplied all the flowers on a consignment basis. They were absolutely gorgeous as she has excellent taste and wonderful arranging ability. Many of her creations were superb, and with the addition of potpourri they created a distinctly luxurious ambiance in the store. My problem however was this:

Despite me weighing two hundred pounds and looking like the battle-scarred veteran that I am, I was continually being asked if I did the flowers. None of the ladies seemed convinced when I

I was continually being asked if I did the flowers.

Decorate with them, sell them, and use them to add color, interest and ambiance.

told them that I did not. It became a standing joke among my friends and staff and used to add a lighthearted moment to many a dull day. Maybe I should have said that I did. It might have increased sales!

Mirrors

These are to see yourself in. Wrong!

They are to make your booth look bigger. Hung at the right angle and height they do just that. Put one at either end or in the middle, vary their heights, and your booth looks bigger from either end or from the middle.

Wooden framed ones, gilt framed ones, steel framed ones, and Art Deco ones—they are all excellent selling, decorative pieces. They also go well with dining room sets, living room sets, dens, and bedroom arrangements. Stick to antique ones only, if you can.

In the illustrations (see pp. 85 and 91, for example) you will see a large French gilt mirror that was absolutely gorgeous. It is the type of product that does well for me and should do well for you also. As you can see, it has all the qualities that you and I are looking for: It is antique, unusual, and very pretty.

It had one other unique feature. Being so large, it was slightly flexible and came with a stiffening bar at the back that you could leave on or off. The lady that bought it had a large entrance hall that faced the sun. This gave her a problem. She wanted a mirror, but since they are flat, the reflection almost blinded you as you walked in after midday.

My flexible one solved her problem. By leaving out the stiffening bar, the center of the mirror bowed out away from the wall about three inches, and the two side mirrors then angled left and right slightly. Presto! No direct reflection into your eyes when you came to lunch! Her friends now visit more often. I sold it for a good price too!

Lamps

The second best kept decorating secret. I don't care what you are selling in your new business—add lamps. How many dealers do? Not many. And for goodness' sake, **keep them switched on all the time**. Don't be so cheap. How can you sell an unlit lamp? I don't know … yet I see them in booths all the time.

Positioning lamps caused the mirror and bowl to sparkle.

Table lamps, floor lamps, chandeliers, and wall lamps should all be used for decorative effect. Anne Slade, who works for me, is very good at using them. I saw her display a lovely cut glass punch bowl by setting it on a flat mirror in the middle of a dark oak buffet. Positioning two of my Japanese porcelain lamps on either side and slightly above caused the mirror and bowl to sparkle like diamonds. Most effective! (See illustration above.)

Remember: Don't just position the lamp, look at its light pattern and use it to highlight pictures, porcelain, or a piece of furniture.

Now I'm going to break one of my own rules. You can too, now that you are almost a professional.

Finding old antique lamps is very difficult. Buy them when you can. As an alternative, go to market or your lamp wholesaler and find some high quality reproductions, particularly small ones retailing at about $40.

I sell antique-style bronze hummingbird lamps, tulip lamps, and fluted lamps—all good quality reproductions. As long as they have that quality look and are not just cheap Far Eastern products, they will sell. Be sure to mark them as antique replica lamps. I like lamps and highly recommend you sell them too. They don't take up space, they enhance your furniture, and they make that cash till ring!

Old lace! Use it to decorate dining tables, halltrees, wardrobes, and the corner of that beautiful antique buffet.

Old lace

The third best kept secret in the antique business. Buy some old lace tablecloths and bedspreads. Use them to decorate dining tables, halltrees, wardrobes, and the corner of that beautiful antique buffet. They don't take up space and are another good seller. Make sure that they are antique—there are enough of them around. If you get short of them, put a small ad in the paper and you will get flooded with offers. It's the type of thing that ladies hand down from mother to daughter to granddaughter, and the type of item they sell when short of cash.

Rugs and throws

Hung over the edge of chairs, they look just great. Cat and horoscope designs are very popular. An impulse buy, they maximize your sales per square foot. Since antique throws are almost impossible to find, new throws labeled as such add color. Rugs, in turn, break up the carpeting and set off the furniture.

They both add money to the cash till.

"That's the bit I like."

Don't we all!

Pictures

Pictures are great sellers and produce maximum profit. Try to get antique ones and mix them with tasteful new ones. I always think that antique dealers miss a great opportunity by not realizing that they are antique dealers and interior decorators.

The big criteria when buying pictures is to judge your customer base. Heavy gilt-framed antique pictures are sought by wealthy customers, while country scenes, flower arrangements, and sea scenes are popular in the mid-price range. When buying new pictures, make sure that they are of conservative, tasteful subjects and that the frames look to be of quality. Let me tell you of "Milan's folly," as my friends call it.

On a trip to England I saw some very unusual chalk-drawn pictures of nudes. They were being auctioned at an antique auction and the artist was a local celebrity in Hungerford, England.

Following my maxim of judging my customer base, I figured that some of my thirty-year-old pilot friends would love them. I did … so why wouldn't they? Sure, they were a little way out, but thirty-year-old pilots are supposed to be a little wild, right?

Would anyone like to buy three very tasteful, chalk-drawn, nude pictures? I'll sell them cheap!

Display your pictures with other wall decorations. Too many pictures make Jack a dull boy.

Stick to conservative scenes. Flowers, sea scenes, battleships, old cottages, horses, cats, and rabbits will do fine. No nudes!

One final thing: Space your pictures with other wall decorations. Too many pictures make Jack a dull boy. Mix in plates, clocks, small wall cabinets, and old telephones.

"Why?"

Because you have to keep the customer interested. Breaking up the pictures adds contrast and keeps their minds thinking about alternatives. They might realize that the wall clock is a better bet for the husband's den than the seascape.

It's also more expensive and carries a bigger profit!

Other accessories

One word sums up accessories: unusual. Only buy unusual accessories and buy as big a variety as possible.

Here are some ideas: vases, crystal punch bowls, wooden boxes, ashtrays, quality porcelain, bronze statues, silver tea and coffee sets, glass and silver butter dishes, salt and pepper sets, full crystal and silver cruet sets, old teapots, figurines, walking sticks, antique golf clubs, fruit bowls, and antique liquor sets.

Most popular price points are $10-20, $50-100, and up to $300. Just remember, set up your booth to resemble one of the rooms in your house. Decorate your antique furniture with appropriate accessories and you'll do fine (silver coffee set with a buffet, not with a bedroom suite).

Since you change out your booth or store every three to four weeks, bring out the items that did not previously sell. Your customers will think that it's new inventory and that you are doing such good business that they simply must buy from you.

Everyone loves a winner!

Pillows

These are great as decorative items and just as great as impulse buys. Old, good quality pillows are few and far between, however. Don't buy tatty ones. No one wants them and they do you a great disservice. The alternative is new ones.

If you do decide to sell new ones, make sure that they fit in with the antique look. Pillows with frills are perfect and tapestry ones are a safe bet. Please don't sell blue and white striped ones!

The other thing to remember with pillows is to tailor your sizes to your customer base. Large expensive ones go well with wealthy clients and smaller ones fit mid-income pockets. I personally think that it's better to specialize in one or the other so that you make a statement that sticks in the buying public's mind.

Pillows, like rugs and small reproduction antique-like lamps, keep the cash till ringing when sales are slow. They are easily reordered and that all-important cash flow is maintained, even if the profit is lower.

Pillows, like rugs and small reproduction antique-like lamps, keep the cash till ringing when sales are slow.

Talking of profit, many of the new items I have mentioned above will not bear your 2.5 multiple. Be happy with a 100 to 125 percent mark-up, but only on the new items. You are using them to build up your sales per square foot and not as your primary business. Maintain the 2.5 factor on any antique ones, as customers understand that antique lamps, rugs, and pillows are a rare commodity. They will be prepared to pay more for them. When you get some, charge a lot. They are difficult to come by.

Ironwork

Ornamental gates, crosses, shelves, and flower stands are terrific accessories to sell with antique furniture and pictures. The see-through aspect of wrought-iron seems to enhance the solid bulk of most pieces of antique furniture.

But beware! Only buy old ironwork.

Decorate your antique furniture with appropriate accessories and you'll do fine.

"How can I tell if it's old? It all looks rusty to me."

Easy. Old wrought-iron has the decorative shapes cast, not hand bent. New wrought-iron is mostly strip plate twisted and turned. The cost of labor has made it prohibitive to cast and form new designs. All you have to do, therefore, is buy ironwork with cast pieces welded to the main frame. This ensures that it's relatively

Display the silver coffee set with the buffet, not with the bedroom suite.

old. This is only a guide, because some cast iron still comes from Mexico and China. Small pieces are harder to identify as antiques because many of these are still foundry cast today. Use your head and look for the "Made in China" labels. If you see them and the item is still pretty, knock the dealer's price down by half.

Two items of ironwork stick in my mind. One is the cemetery cross from Lourdes, France, and the other is four gates that my friend Beverly found at a flea market. The gates were purchased by a dealer in Macon, Georgia, who made them into tables by having legs welded to them. Adding a large glass top, she had herself four very unusual antique coffee tables. It was a wonderful idea.

Potpourri!

I always remember a writer friend telling me that writing was all about describing the senses. Sight, touch, taste, and smell were the keys he said, and the more you felt these, the better writer you became. Thank you, Warren!

The same goes for selling antiques.

We have seen color, touched frills on pillows, rugs, etc., and tasted the free coffee your well-run mall gives to customers.

But what about smell?

If we get three out of four we are batting .75, aren't we?

The fourth best kept secret in the antiques business is potpourri.

"But it costs so much!"

Nonsense. Go to the deodorizer section in your local grocery store and buy potpourri. No, not the bathroom atomizer type or the plug-in type. What you need is the little vial-of-oil type that costs about a dollar. Buy the "rose" smell—it's not so strong. Now put a few drops into the flower arrangements that you have decorating the dining room table and buffet. Once a week is enough. Not only will the flower arrangements sell faster, but your booth will leave an indelible impression on all the customers that come into it. It will also draw them away from the other areas.

Sometimes a little money goes a long way! But be prepared, customers will want to buy the potpourri from you. I couldn't sell it. After all, how could I tell them that I use a cheap oil instead of an exclusive and expensive French brand? They would never have bought that $18,000 Georgian bookcase if I had told them that.

Labels

Talking of the $18,000 Georgian bookcase brings to mind the fifth best kept antiques secret: labels. Pricing labels that is.

"But they are just pricing labels."

The $18,000 Georgian bookcase

Labels! Time and again I have seen ladies spend hours just reading them.

Absolutely not. That's only a minor purpose of labels. The main one is information.

One of your most effective sales tools is to write as much information on the price tags as you can. You can't have enough. Time and time again, I have seen ladies spend hours in my store just reading them. It makes them feel part of the business. It also gives your booth an air of professionalism.

"Where do I get all this information to write on the labels?"

Here's where:

1. *Off the piece itself.* Describe all its interesting features in detail. For example, "Note the beautiful fleur-de-lis pattern on the headboard." You may think they can see that for themselves, but if you don't believe me, try it. See how often they call their companions over and say, "Look at the fleur-de-lis pattern on the headboard!"

2. *From the dealer, auctioneer, or private seller.* Ask, ask, and ask again. Carry a pocket tape-recorder and record the answers. Put all the details on the label, no matter how mundane.

3. *From research.* Use *Collins, Millers,* etc. to find equivalent pieces and note their descriptions. Use similar wording. My Georgian bookcases sell better when I attach an essay to them. Place of purchase, history of the area, details of people's occupations (farmers, tradespeople, etc.), and distinguishing features of the piece are all in it. You will be surprised how many people don't know that old glass has a wavy finish until you see them step back and view it from side to side. Unless you point out the old glass, they won't even notice it.

Use the labels as a sales tool and a price tag. It takes a lot of time but is well worth it.

Those five hours a week I mentioned at the beginning are starting to look more like ten. I didn't know then whether you had it in you to be a professional, so I had to fudge a little, but now I know you can handle it.

Spotlights

Spotlights can be used to great effect in a booth to highlight wall decorations or pictures. Since most booths are only ten feet wide, I recommend that you use floor spots. Surprisingly, they complement your lamp lighting without detracting from that warm, cozy look. Highlighting an item with spots usually sells it faster. Do it!

$ $ $ $ $

By covering each of the decorative methods and products above, I have gotten you into an inquiring frame of mind. I have also convinced you to put as much thought and planning into the layout of your booth as you normally put into buying and selling products. It will make you a well-rounded antique professional. Too many dealers buy products and then simply put them into any available space without any thought whatsoever. That's the reason why so many people think of antiques as junk.

If more dealers set up their booths attractively, we would all have a larger slice of the buying population's interest in decorating their homes. They would purchase our type of merchandise instead of buying at the furniture and decorating

Finally, one very important aspect. I let my furniture, ironworks, vases, etc. be my props.

chains. Do your part. Every little bit helps and is essential if you want to keep growing and earning more of that money!

There is one further aspect that I would like to cover. I call it **positioning your merchandise**.

First a question. Why do ninety percent of the dealers only see the rectangular shape of their booths? Why must that writing desk always be positioned flat against the wall and not at an angle across the corner?

"Because it takes up too much space at an angle and leaves a useless area behind it," I hear them say. Note the use of them and not you! You're getting too smart now to be lumped in with the crowd.

So why don't you put a standard lamp into that space and hang a matched pair of facing pictures to fill it up? When walking up the aisle, don't you see that corner first? Surely a good first impression is all-important, just like in a job interview.

If it catches their eye, customers will walk right by the intervening booths to get a look at yours. Use psychology to hook them first. Don't let them spend their money elsewhere!

Finally, one very important aspect. If you've read everything I've written, you will have noticed that I use no props. I don't believe in them. I let my furniture, ironworks, vases, etc. be my props.

A very astute dealer once said this about my store: "Everything in there is for sale. It's all home decoration or furniture. He could sell everything and simply shut the door … there would be nothing else to take out."

My answer was: "Why should I spend money on dead merchandise when I have the finest props available in salable product?"

When I feel cheeky I also add, "You can even buy me!"

Chapter 8 review

1. Put as much **thought into decorating your booth** as you now do into buying and selling merchandise.

2. **Use color**! In painting the walls, in bright carpeting, and in selling colorful merchandise.

3. Cheat! **Use the magazines and paint store decorators for free ideas and advice**.

4. Booth position. **Get the first in line**. If not, a corner one with eight-foot pegboard for hanging pictures will do. As a third choice, the one near the bathrooms is just as good.

5. Use flowers, mirrors, lamps, old lace, rugs, pictures, accessories, pillows, wrought-iron, and that wonderful "rose" smell to **build ambiance, draw customers, and increase your sales per square foot**. Don't forget that labels are a sales tool too. They hold the customer enthralled in your booth or store.

$$\$ \ \$ \ \$ \ \$$$

Finally, remember that you don't have to spend money on props. You have the finest available in your own merchandise.

Is life good or what?

9. Paperwork

Stop sweating. I'm no Harvard educated accountant either and I hate paperwork as much as you do. Figures don't lie, however, and we must have them because they are certainly better than our instincts in telling us the state of our business. Being the professionals that we are, we are just going to have to grit our teeth and bear it.

When I first thought about this very important chapter, I decided to use the services of an accountant to write it. That was after I thought of leaving it out altogether. Being the maverick that I am, I realized that the first course of action was being chicken, and the second, a cop-out. So here goes. "How to run your accounts the easy way and still know what's happening."

Being the simpleton that I am, I split my accounts into five sections. I know that some of you might actually be accountants, but please keep your suggestions to yourselves. This is for me and my fellow garden-variety human beings.

In order for my five journal accounting system to work, all you have to do is **keep it up weekly, if not daily**. It is based on what is actually happening and not on some nebulous projections, and as such, it breaks down instantly if not maintained.

My five journals are as follows:

1. A monthly sales journal
2. A monthly purchase journal
3. A yearly inventory journal
4. A layaway journal
5. An overhead ledger

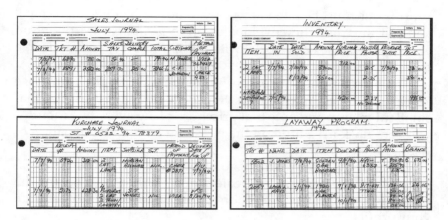

Simple sales, inventory, purchase and layaway journals

When deciding on these five journals, I only took the taxes applicable to Texas into consideration. I realize that in other states and in other parts of the world, bureaucracy has a far heavier hand. The thought of 17.5 percent Value Added Tax (VAT) in England sends shivers down my spine. The point is, for someone just starting out, all you need to do is maintain a simple record of what you are doing. Nothing is firm, so modify it to suit yourself. Later on, pay an accountant to do your books. It's far easier.

Sales journal

Get yourself a lined book as per my sample. Write in every sale, or if in a booth, every time you get your printout from the mall's owner. This will usually be twice a month, i.e. around the 15th and the 30th. At the end of the month, rule off the columns and add totals to give yourself an overall picture. Keep this record for next year's planning. Not only does it give you the state of your business, but also what is selling. This enables you to buy intelligently at the next auction or estate sale, or from the newspaper. That wardrobe you saw being advertised will be a good buy if your record shows that at the same time last year, wardrobes were a hot selling item. It also gives you the best price points at which to buy and sell. Look back at your previous purchases and sales for exact figures.

Monthly purchase journal

This one must be filled in weekly, if not daily. Keep all receipts and put them into an envelope or on to a clipboard. I prefer an envelope because I can label it with the applicable month and have those all important records for you-know-who (yes, the I.R.S.).

The most important reason for keeping a monthly purchase journal is to pick up trends. If you check your purchases of that small tulip lamp and note that prices are rising every two months, you can mark up a little on the ones you have in anticipation of rising replacement costs.

If you didn't know that's good policy, don't scold yourself. Ninety-nine percent of the dealers don't either. It is one of the most important factors in eroding your mark-up, and therefore your profits.

Use the purchasing record for tons and tons of information. For example: Remember that decision buying price we talked about when going to the auction? Now that you have a purchase journal you can look up what the last buffet cost you and not just use your multiple factor. You can base your purchase of the new one on hard figures. Using your acumen, your multiple factor, and a definite price must be better than just relying on your ability alone.

The other use for a purchase journal is to control your cash outflow. By keeping a running total, you can see if you are overspending your budget. Remember the basis we used for establishing your multiple factor in Chapter 6 and the purchasing budget total?

"$8,600, wasn't it?"

Yes, that's right. That amount was your yearly purchasing budget for a $20,000 sales target. By adding up your monthly purchases, you will be able to control this cash and stay within your budgeted figure.

Yearly inventory journal

How much do you have invested?

"I don't really know," is what most dealers will tell you.

Add up your inventory—that's if you have a record. I know

it's not strictly true, as layaways, items on hold, and purchases awaiting delivery should be taken into consideration, but it's accurate enough for you. In any case, you will need an income statement (called a profit and loss statement in England) every three months.

"Income statement every three months!"

Yes. But don't sweat it. With the sales journal, purchase journal, and overhead ledger, it is relatively easy. Just take your sales, deduct the cost of the sold items to get your gross profit, and then deduct the three months' overhead total to get net profit.

Voila! Easy wasn't it? (There's that French word again.)

As in the other journals, your inventory journal is loaded with information. Not only can it help you establish a decision buying price for tonight's auction, but it also tells you whether you should purchase that buffet or not. If you still have two in stock and they haven't sold for three months, don't buy another one. Bid on the halltree instead. A quick rundown of your inventory journal before going to the auction previewing will help tremendously in deciding what you might be interested in.

For fast selling items, your inventory journal can help you plan ahead so that you will be ready for a sales rush.

In Grapevine we have two yearly festivals, Mainstreet Days in May, and Grapefest in September. Grapefest draws the richer crowd. Something to do with the wine tasting, I think. By checking my inventory in the first week of August, I can make sure that I have plenty of those tulip lamps in stock for the Grapefest weekend. You would be surprised how many customers buy them when slightly inebriated.

It's really quite easy to operate. Just fill it in every time you buy something. Not that difficult, is it?

Do it now—not after the football game!

Layaway journal

A must, to avoid trouble. It also stops you from looking foolish when layaway customers come in to pay without their sales ticket. All you have to do then is look it up. Makes you feel smug, doesn't it? And rightly so. You're a professional.

The layaway journal's best feature, however, is that it keeps the cash flowing in. Check it weekly and call up any customer who is delinquent.

One other use for the layaway journal is to keep you cheerful.

"To keep me cheerful? How's that?"

Well, when your bank balance is low and the light bill is due, just check your journal and start calling. If no one is due to pay today, just eat bread and water until next week when the next layaway payment comes in. Then go back to sirloin steaks again!

Seriously though, it also helps when a customer calls and wants to cancel her payment agreement and get a refund. The agreement she signed, together with your record, will ensure that you don't end up out-of-pocket, as the English say.

Overhead ledger

This is the easy one to keep up. After all, the rent stays the same. Sure, but remember that you had to make that extra long journey to pick up that table, and while on that trip you blew a tire? That's an overhead expense. How about that stain you had to buy for that desk? Yes, I know it's recorded as a purchase, but it's also an extra overhead expense. So is that insurance payment, those rags, that polish, etc.

The best way to operate this system is to record your merchandise purchases in your purchase journal and your operating expenses in the overhead journal.

Income statement

Do you want to know if you are making a profit?

Before you answer that question, think about it. Are you running your business because you want and need the income, or are you just doing it to keep yourself busy, because you enjoy the company, or because you like being around antiques?

Sounds silly, doesn't it? Yet you'd be surprised how many dealers I've met who actually say to me, "I'm doing it for fun." Fun to me means partying, going deep sea fishing, or traveling; certainly not running an antique business. That's not to say that it's not fun, it's just that it's a business first.

For those of you who run your business only for fun, forget about profit and loss. You'd rather not know, and I envy you.

For those that are serious and run your business for fun and profit, you must know every three months, if not every month, what your position is.

So add up the sales from your sales journal, deduct your purchase journal total, and then deduct your overhead as detailed in your overhead journal. This gives you your net profit. I seem to remember telling you this before. It's important, so follow my advice.

Work those figures. Do it! And don't cheat. You need to know, if you are serious about your business. If not, play and have fun, but be prepared to dig into your own pocket.

Taxes

What a horrible word.

I don't want to talk about taxes, save to say:

- Keep an accurate record.
- If possible, put the money into a separate account.
- Pay them.

You know more about your own local taxes than I do, so I won't cover this in detail. If you don't know what they are, ask other dealers or your local tax office. In most malls, the management deducts the sales tax before paying you your check and sends it directly to the tax office. This is a good system because it deducts the money right away and saves you the responsibility later on. If the management doesn't do this, call your local tax office to get the forms and find out your responsibilities.

Borrowing money

To borrow money in the antique business is as difficult as in any other business. If you do so, just remember to spend it on inventory only. Don't buy a new car or TV. You can do that once you have sold the inventory.

We have reached the end of this chapter. It wasn't much fun, but figures are a necessary evil. Knowing the state of your business is essential to your success.

Chapter 9 review

1. **Set up five simple journals**. A sales, purchase, inventory, layaway, and overhead journal will do to start.

2. **Keep them up-to-date**.

3. Use the information in them to **purchase at the right price** and for **planning ahead**.

4. Do an **income statement** every three months.

5. **Keep the layaway journal up-to-date**. Chase customers who are late to keep your cash flow on track.

6. Taxes! What an ugly word. **Deduct them from your sales and deposit them in a separate account**. Pay them on time.

7. **Borrow money for inventory alone**.

$$\$\ \$\ \$\ \$\ \$$$

I'm glad this chapter's over. Believe me, I hate paperwork as much as you do, but to be a responsible dealer, you have to keep it up. If you don't know the state of your business, you won't be in business long.

Let's move on to product mix, a much more interesting subject, don't you think?

10. Product Mix and Trends

We are not in the antique business, we are in the home decorating business.

"Why do you say that? This book is called *Money from Antiques*."

That's right, but most dealers think that there is a mystique about antiques that will rub off on customers. Wrong! Most customers are just looking to decorate or spruce up their homes and prefer the idea of furniture and accessories with character. The thought of mass-produced products turns them off, and so they come to us. It has nothing to do with mystique; it has everything to do with character. Since antique pieces are all unique and have their own individuality, our competition is not among ourselves but from the large contemporary furniture stores.

The most important thing that we can learn from our competition is that they display their furniture together with accessories in a **home type setting**. How many of us do that? Not many, that's for sure. Just look in any mall and you will see that only about one in ten booths looks anything like a room in your house. Modern furniture stores on the other hand, are interior decorating stores. They carry lamps, rugs, pictures, and statues, as well as furniture. That's what we have to do.

They display their furniture together with accessories in a "home type setting."

I personally shy away from calling my store an antique store. The name Kings does not indicate antiques. When asked, I say that we are an interior decorating and accent furniture store.

"Why? Are you ashamed of antiques?"

Quite the contrary. I love them, but to be in antiques is to be in business first and in antiques second. Here's a thought.

If you asked one hundred people how many are interested in antiques, how many would say they are? Twenty percent maybe?

On the other hand, if you asked one hundred people how many are interested in home accessories or furniture, I'd bet that seventy percent would say they are.

By calling ourselves purely antique dealers, we are immediately cutting ourselves off from another fifty percent of the potential buyers. We compound this by setting up our booths as junk shows and then expect our customer traffic to increase.

Well, I don't, and I don't think you should either.

So let's copy the successful furniture and accessory stores. Let's set up our booths to reflect our own personality, as we do when setting up our living room, den, family room, or bedroom. The nicer the better ... and a bit of coziness also helps.

Here's a tip: Find out if there is a design district in your area where local interior decorators go to shop. Visit it and check out the showrooms. You'll be surprised at how many ideas you can pick up to help you decorate your booth.

Here's another tip: Make a friend of an interior decorator that shops with you. Give her an extra five percent discount to help you plan and set up your booth. Not only will you get valuable advice, but you will get free training as well.

Product mix

Set up a dining room arrangement, living room setting, or bedroom scene. Decorate it with the lamps, pictures, or the rugs you would expect to find there. Change it out every four to five weeks and sell, sell, and sell. It's a simple secret, but one that many dealers never think about.

"What if I don't have a full arrangement and have to control my purchases?"

Then make a statement. Put all the bureaus you have into your booth at the same time. Or all your washstands. Or all your halltrees and chests. **Make it look like you planned it**. That's what I mean by product mix.

Use combinations to attract attention. If you don't have that many bureaus, use the ones you have and load them with all those vases you recently bought. **Make a statement with your product mix**. It's almost, but not quite, as good as a room setting.

Where to find ideas? All around you—in your own mall, in the nearby malls. Also in the nearby furniture stores, in restaurants (look around—they employ in-house interior decorators), in your friends' homes, in builders' show houses, and in magazines.

Yes, in magazines. The shelves in bookstores are full of them. How about the local library? Check out the shelf with interior decorating books.

What's the purpose of all this?

To sell, sell, and sell some more, of course.

If it's displayed well, it will sell. If it's thrown together haphazardly it'll turn the customer off. Few of us can imagine what that side table will look like in our white carpeted family room if it's in the back of the booth covered by old Coca-Cola bottles. On the other hand, set out in front of the booth with a nice lace doily and a porcelain lamp on it, it is a completely different story.

8 x 4 foot wooden trellises hung beneath the lights give the room an ambiance of its own.

I once went into an old western type restaurant in Plano, north Dallas. It was quite hideous inside. To hide the ugly ceiling the owner had hung some of those criss-crossed wooden 8 x 4 foot trellises below it. You know the ones—you nail them to your house wall to hold the climbing plants. I liked the idea. It was simple and cheap (most good ideas are) and also highly effective. At the time I was setting up a romantic-type clothes section in my store and needed to give the section a look of its own.

Solution: I bought two of the trellises from the local hardware store and painted them peach. They cost $8 each. Then I hung them below the strip lights in that section with brown hemp rope (also from the hardware store), leaving the knots clearly visible. They diffused the light nicely, gave the area a softer glow, and even though the section was in a big room, it gave the corner an ambiance all of its own. Cheap but effective.

Trends 'n' fads

Trends are in, fads are out.

One gives you time to capitalize on it and sell more, and the other comes and goes so quickly that most of us are not even aware of the latest craze. Trends result in longer term business and fads usually result in you holding a lot of dead stock.

"What should I look for in trends?"

Do you remember those magazines I talked about? Well, they set the trends. Keep an eye on them. They influence what's in and what's out. When you see them pushing pine furniture, buy that antique pine hutch at the auction. Put a chair next to it and place two earth-tone-colored tapestry pillows on it. Yes, I know that they had tan pillows in that picture in *Interiors* magazine. Congratulations on picking that up. Did you notice the dry flowers hanging from that grill above the bed? Again earth-tone colors.

Puzzled?

"What does this have to do with antiques?"

We are an interior decorating and antique business, remember? Use the same type of flowers to help you sell that hutch. An arrangement positioned on one corner will do nicely. It will catch that interior decorator's eye as soon as she visits your booth and may sell that hutch right then and there.

I try to pick up on trends as soon as I can, but success seems to elude me quite often. The first I usually know of what's in, is when a customer comes in clutching a torn magazine page in her hand. It's guaranteed that I don't have the same occasional table that is in the picture. In this case, take the trouble to take her name and number; you never know if you will see it in a nearby mall or at the auction. Call her back if you do, make a deal with the owner, and bingo! … another sale.

This happened to me with a glass-topped metal table. They are quite difficult to find, so when the customer asked me to look out for one, I didn't have much hope. Dang! Would you believe that they had one at the very next auction I went to. The bidding was high, but because I had a definite buyer I was able to get it. The customer was a lawyer and was prepared to pay just that little bit more. Chalk up one satisfied customer!

So take note of trends. They are usually around long enough so that you can take advantage of them and make it worth your while. Just forget the fads.

Seasons

I know, you think I'm going to talk about Christmas first. Wrong! I'm going to talk about summer first.

"Why summer?"

Because those dog days of summer are the worst period in the antique business calendar. Vacations, children out of school, the heat—everything conspires to keep the customers away from spending money. Those months from June to August in particular seem to drag on forever and business takes on a whole different aspect.

"Can I do something about it?"

Sure you can.

The first thing is to understand why this period is so slow: obviously because the customers are away, or are spending their hard earned dollars on other things. Vacations, as you are aware, cost money. So do school supplies and new clothes. That doesn't mean that they don't have any spending money at all though, just that they have less of it. Many of them will still come into your booth to browse, it's just that they won't reach for their checkbooks at the drop of a hat.

"So how can we maximize sales, in view of the customer's other financial commitments?"

By having a larger amount of lower cost merchandise. Note that I said lower cost and not cheaper. In summer we have to go for volume, rather than high profits on larger, more expensive products. To do so, we obviously have to anticipate the slow sales period and procure lower-value merchandise early in the new year.

Here I want to ask you a question. Do you have any experience with the gift industry?

No? In the gift and household furniture business, all the main trade shows are held in January or February and also in June or July. The reason for this is that orders are placed then, to cater for the slow summer months and also for busy winter ones. In other words, the gift and mainstream furniture industries plan six months ahead. Take a leaf out of their books and plan for the slow and busy periods well ahead of time.

The other idea you can implement is to have special sales. Just think of the department stores and their huge summer sales. Since we have already built in a discount factor, we can use sales to maintain cash flow. A word of caution however: Don't overuse the sale tactic. It can backfire. Make your sale for a specific time only and then remove the sale tags. If you don't, you will have customers asking for the discount forever.

Plates, silverware, candlesticks, lamps, and other unusual items sell well during slow months.

In the higher $100 to $150 price range, small occasional tables do well.

You can now see why I dealt with summer first. It's the slow months that sink you, not the busy Christmas ones. Anticipate the slow period and plan for it. It is crucial that you do.

"So what kind of merchandise shall I put in my booth for summer?"

Any small, good quality accessories under $50, or smaller furniture pieces around $100 to $150.

Bearing this in mind, plates, silverware, candlesticks, small lamps, throws, rugs, and other unusual items sell well. If they fall into the price points indicated above, customers will buy them as personal gifts. All these are around the $50 mark.

In the higher $100 to $150 price range, small occasional tables, antique mirrors (both wall hanging and vanity top ones) do well, as do small chests, plant stands, and pictures.

Any small, good quality accessories under $50, or smaller furniture pieces around $100 to $150

By making sure that you have a larger amount of these kinds of products in your booth during summer, you will maintain your sales level as high as possible, while others are suffering cash flow problems.

As professionals, we have to take a hint from the gift and household furniture dealers and start purchasing these types of items in February, March, and April. By cutting back on the larger or more expensive products, we can tilt our inventory towards the more salable ones. If you make a conscious effort to do so, you will increase your cash reserves while having faster selling merchandise available for the slow summer period.

I always remember how nerve-wracking it was before I actually realized that I could do something about this slow period. It only came to me when I saw how many lamps, rugs, throws, and candlesticks we were selling for cash, and how many large furniture pieces were being put on layaway. Even though I had known why the trade shows were held in their respective months since I had been involved in the gift and furniture businesses as a consultant, I hadn't really believed it.

To test my theory I rented a booth in July in a nearby mall. Imagine my surprise when I sold more in the first week in that booth than I had in my high-end shop. I became an instant convert. Remember this lesson. It cost me money; it doesn't need to cost you anything. The sign of a professional is when you start planning your business, instead of just following the herd. Anticipate the slow months, change your inventory to lower cost products, and keep the cash flowing when others are crying.

Now to Christmas

Obviously the best selling period in the whole year. Christmas in the antique business covers the whole spectrum of price points. The months of October and November should find you product heavy and cash poor. It is also the period when your five hours of work a week start to increase. In the three-week period before Christmas, plan to spend every minute you can in your booth. The more you talk to customers looking for just the right Christmas present, the more likely they are to buy your merchandise and not your competitors'. It is also the best period to build up your customer base by injecting your personality into your business.

Here are a few other things you can do:
1. Decorate your booth with lights and a small Christmas tree.
2. Take special care in positioning your lamps. Make the place look cozy.
3. Give a special Christmas present with each item purchased. Every Christmas I give away a very nice, but cheap, Christmas tree ornament with every sale. It's not the item, but the thought, that sticks in your customer's mind.
4. Offer to wrap any accessory purchased. Since you should be in your booth every evening those last three weeks, put up a sign saying "Free gift-wrapping service is available from 7 to 9 PM every day." You will, of course, have to buy a supply of boxes and paper, but your multiple factor took this into consideration. Remember we rounded it out from 2.3 to 2.5?

In conclusion, I know that you understand the importance of the Christmas sales period. Maximize it by planning ahead. It is the most profitable season of the whole year. Once it's over, go on vacation. Just don't bother me if you see me sunning myself on the beach. After Christmas I don't want to know anything about antiques for at least a few weeks. Okay, okay! For a few days anyway.

Special days

Valentine's Day, Mother's Day, Father's Day and Thanksgiving Day—all are great for the gift industry. I have never found them to be especially good for the antique business. Because of this, I have never done anything special for these days and don't seem to have lost out on sales. If they want a Father's Day present, they will come in and buy those antique golf clubs or that antique clock they looked at weeks before. Offer to wrap it up nicely if you are there when they pick it up.

Chapter 10 review

You are not in the antique business. If you are serious, you are in the interior decorating and antique furniture business. Don't

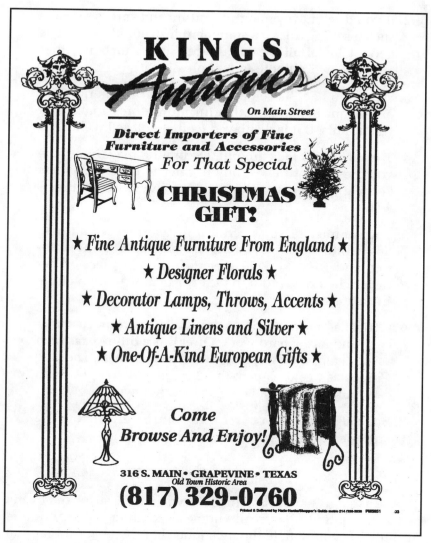

Christmas is for terrific sales.

cut yourself off from that seventy percent of the population who treat antique accessories and furniture purely as accent pieces.

1. **Set up your booth or store in a planned setting** just like you would in your own house. Dining rooms, bedrooms, and living rooms don't have a mish-mash of items; they all fit in with the room's use.

2. If you don't have enough furniture and smalls to make such a setting, **make a statement** instead. It's almost as good. Cluster all the same types of products together and make your booth look professional.

3. Where do I get those **decorating ideas**? In interior decorating magazines, in other furniture stores, malls, and restaurants. If it is displayed well, it will sell well.

4. **Trends are in, fads are out**. Decorating magazines give you the current trends. Buy to cater to those customers keeping up-to-date with fashions. Antiques fit trends well.

5. The summer season is critical for your sales and cash flow. Anticipate it and **stock up on small $50 accessories and $100 to $150 accent furniture pieces**. Stay cash rich and spend it in October in anticipation of the Christmas rush.

6. Christmas is for terrific sales, building your customer base, and lots of hard work. **Offer those little extras** such as gift wrapping during the hours you are there. The little Christmas tree ornament that I suggested you give with each purchase will build you a loyal following.

7. **Special days don't require much effort in the antiques business**. Rather, look longer term.

$ $ $ $ $

At this stage, I know that many of you will be surprised by my belief that antiques are really home decorating accessories and furniture. It will deflate the mystique slightly. Don't forget that you are in business first, and in antiques second. In any case, antiques have such individuality of their own that they never lose their fascination. Have fun selling them, but make money as well.

11. Building a Customer Base

What is a customer base and how do I build it?

The phrase intrigued and puzzled me when I first heard it and it was only later, when I could put faces and products to the words, that I understood it more. I then realized how essential it was to success in the antique business, or to any retail business for that matter. It was a beautiful, elderly lady called Mildred, who actually explained her buying philosophy to me and cleared up what **customer base** meant. In simple terms, she elaborated on why she enjoyed visiting my shop and buying from us. This is what she said:

"I come into your shop because you always carry interesting merchandise that suites my tastes, and because you fuss over me and make me feel special."

Let's think about what she said. First, she came in because we carried suitable products and second, because we made a fuss over her.

Loyal customers like Mildred are your customer base.

If more and more of them visit your booth regularly, your customer base will increase, as will your sales and cash. When it's large enough, the sales to these loyal, regular customers will carry you through the quiet months. So … your customer base is, in fact, also your cash flow base.

"I have a booth in a mall and can't always be there, so how can I fuss over them?" I can hear your question already.

You can fuss over them by doing the following:

1. Have a customer register for them to fill in with sections for their name, address, the product they bought from you, plus any comments.
2. Send them a small thank you card. Address it to them by full name.
3. Occasionally send them the same card offering a ten percent discount on their next purchase in appreciation of their past business.

It's being fussed over that customers like. It makes them feel special. I know it takes time, but believe me, it's well worth it. Mildred once asked me to buy a rug rack she had seen in another mall for her, rather than buying it there herself. I got a dealer's discount, resold it to her for the full price, and turned a profit in half an hour. An easy way to make good money, wasn't it? All because of a little care and attention. She could have bought it there herself, but didn't. It was the fuss that we make over her that counted more than the money!

Remember, there are two reasons for her being so loyal. The first one listed above is that we carry her type of products.

The customer register with columns for the product she bought and for her comments will ensure that you 1) cater to your customers' requirements and tastes, and 2) build relationships.

"What product range should I start with in order to build this customer base?"

Start will the smalls. Items like bedside lamps, Flow Blue plates, silver spoons, antique cookie jars, and even metal city nameplates will do. Just make sure that whatever you choose, the quality and price range suit your intended customer income level. Wealthy customers don't generally buy slightly rusty nameplates, but tradespeople do.

On the other hand, more expensive occasional tables are not a hot seller with plumbers, but great with accountants or professionals. Use your smarts!

Networking with dealers to enlarge your customer base

There are large malls, medium sized malls, and even small malls. In these are unknown dealers, a few known dealers, and in small malls, a family of dealers. They are an important aspect in enlarging your customer base. Your neighboring dealers can help or hinder you in your quest for more loyal customers. If they hinder you, it leads to all of you losing out.

"They're nice people," you say, "they wouldn't hinder me, not them. They wouldn't do anything like that."

Not intentionally, they wouldn't. Unintentionally, they might, by carrying the same type of products as you, so that you all start competing and cutting each other's throats. None of you will make a profit then.

I don't mean furniture, where each buffet is different, but I do mean those small reproduction lamps. If you all start selling them in the same mall, you'll kill that business dead.

"I can see that."

Good. How's this for an idea then:

Since you are now looked upon as a professional by your fellow booth holders, why don't you get together with those around you and each agree to take a risk on one type of product. Can you imagine how many customers you will draw to your special corner of the mall if one of you specializes in crystal, one in majolica, one in silverware, and one in antique bedside lamps? Then, if any of you are at the auction and see a nice crystal vase, bedside lamp, or silver set, you can buy it. For a small commission, your friend can sell it in his or her booth. All of you in turn could do the same and you will all increase your sales by cooperating, instead of competing.

Could be fun!

"Could also be a big headache."

Agreed. But it will build a larger customer base for you all and that's what you want, isn't it?

Discount coupons

I briefly mentioned this under "fussing over customers." I believe that the discount coupon offer should only be used as a very special offer to a particular customer. The scattergun approach is counterproductive in the antique business.

"Why is that?"

Because, as mentioned earlier in the book, the customer is looking for that unique one-off accessory or piece of furniture. If you so much as hint that you are treating them as one of the crowd, they'll run a mile. Don't forget, they look to you as a professional interior decorator specialist, and not a mass market furniture salesman.

Use the discount coupon. Address it directly to Mr. or Mrs. so-and-so. Tell them this only applies to a very few loyal customers. Then ask them if they would like an extra coupon for a special friend.

It will double your customer base in a few short months. If not, I'll buy you dinner when I'm in your city on a book tour. Come to think of it, I might just do that anyway as an appreciation for you buying this book and becoming a professional antique dealer. The more of us the better!

The camera as a sales tool

"What does building a customer base have to do with a camera?"

Well, picture this. Here you are in another mall, on vacation, or just popping into that antique store in Grapevine on your way to your favorite fishing hole. Suddenly you see a red Victorian vase. It rings a bell. Didn't Mildred mention that she needed one in your customer register comments column? Yes, that's where you remember it from.

Out comes your trusty camera. Ask the owner, and ta-daaaa … instant photo. Discuss a dealer's discount, take a business card, and when you get home, send the photo to Mildred. She'll love you for the thought and she'll tell her friend who will also want such special treatment. You just might make some extra cash! All because of one Instamatic shot.

In England, all antique dealers carry their cameras. It's de rigueur, just like their cellular phones.

"De rigueur?"

It means "Required by the current custom or fashion."

My problem with the camera is that I always start out with good intentions, but as soon as I'm in a pile of antiques, I forget that I even have it. Also, I'm impatient and hate fiddling with the focus knob. Maybe that's why most of my photos are hazy.

One final use of the camera that is purely a practical one: When I go on a buying trip, I always photograph the piece that I bought.

Ever the opportunist, I explained that we were doing a photo shoot for this book and asked her whether she would consent to us taking a photo of her taking a photo of the cradle.

If it's a piece of furniture, I often have it delivered later and the photo is a record of what I bought. It ensures that I get the right piece. I also try to pre-sell it from the photo before it actually arrives. I did that with a beautiful mahogany secretary. The lady saw the photograph, gave me a deposit, and bought it the minute it was in the shop. Good business!

While editing this piece, an interesting situation arose in my store. Gerry Grazulis, the professional photographer, my manager Anne Slade, and I were taking photo shots. In the midst of this shambles, with furniture moved aside, stepladders getting in the way, and strip light tubes being removed, a lady came in with a camera and huge telephoto lens hanging around her neck. Brushing past us, she proceeded to take photos of a pine cradle that I had bought at the Pump House in Cardiff, Wales. She needed these to get her out-of-town daughter's approval before buying it.

Ever the opportunist, I explained that we were doing a photo shoot for this book and asked her whether she would consent to us taking a photo of her taking a photo of the cradle. I explained that I needed it for this section. She agreed, but all she could think of was that her hair was not done and that she didn't look her best. She looked good and we managed to convince her so. Hence the photo. Thank you, kind lady.

It just shows how useful the camera can be for you and your customer. It also shows how much fun this business can be!

Using interior decorators to build your customer base

I like interior decorators, but many dealers don't because interior decorators expect, and some almost demand, a discount from you.

"How do I deal with this?"

Professionally!

Most interior decorators consider themselves professionals, even if the training for the job is almost nonexistent. The worthwhile ones will almost always announce themselves as soon as they have found an item that they consider suitable for their customer. If they do, I recommend that right then, upfront, you discuss the discount that would apply to the piece, how much would go to the customer, and when the interior decorator's share would be paid.

The most ideal situation from your point of view is to get the decorator to buy the piece herself, less the full discount. Insist on this if you have any doubt about the deal. This is not always possible, however. If that's the case, write your agreement down on a piece of paper in simple terms and both of you sign it.

Under no circumstances should you let the piece out of your booth without getting paid for it.

Decorators and their clients are notorious for borrowing a piece for the weekend just "to see if it fits." In reality, the client is having an important party and the decorator wants to please her. Since she has already received a commission on the drapes, cushions, carpet, etc., she has no pressing interest in ensuring that her client buys your buffet.

I remember a very sharp lesson:

A well-known decorator selected a very large and grand buffet from my inventory. She wanted to check if it fitted in the space in her client's house. Fortunately, I needed the money and insisted on payment. After considerable discussion, I agreed to take her check, less the discount, and to hold it till Tuesday, this being

Friday. As inducement, the decorator also asked if I would deliver another buffet for the "piano room" and leave it over the weekend. I fell for it and agreed.

While delivering both, I was embarrassed by the argument the two ladies got into. It was obvious that they didn't get on, and I beat a hasty retreat. Before I did, however, I heard the words, "Saturday's party!"

The situation bothered me all weekend, spoiling an otherwise pleasant time. By Tuesday, I was so anxious that I deposited the decorator's check as soon as my bank opened their doors. It was for $2800. To help me, my bank called the issuing bank and requested a verbal clearance, which they got.

Ten minutes later I walked into my shop. Sitting at my desk was the decorator. She told me that her client had changed her mind and would not pay her for the unit, so she wanted her check back.

"You are the proud owner of a very, very grand buffet," I replied.

The roof nearly collapsed!

It took me ten more days to get my other buffet out of the high-powered lawyer's wife's house. Don't let it happen to you!

Good decorators can help you build your customer base. Their clients come back on their own and buy without the discount. If they are that good, decorators come back with their clients and then you don't mind giving the discount. Some expect a fifty percent discount; I never give more than thirty.

The other problem when dealing with decorators is embarrassment. The client expects a discount, the decorator doesn't want you to give one. If you dealt with this professionally at the beginning, as I suggested, you don't have a problem.

"Ten percent, Mrs. Jones," you say, watching a twenty percent sigh of relief cross the decorator's face.

Everybody's happy! Particularly you.

Advertising to build your customer base

Yellow pages, newspaper advertising, flyers, word-of-mouth—all will do.

"What should I spend my money on?"

Word of mouth—it's cheapest and best. The little thank you cards get talked about among friends and do you a world of good!

Yellow pages. Earlier on we discussed yellow pages advertising for buying products. It also obviously works for selling products, but be specific. Ads that are so crowded that you can hardly read them do nothing for me. Besides which, I wear glasses to read and I hate putting them on. Give me big, bold, clear letters telling me something specific and I'll come along just to see what else you have, particularly if you write "Professionally selected merchandise." Don't forget your phone number. Yes, the one we discussed in the chapter on buying merchandise. I know you only have a booth, but I told you that it's worth it. Leave a message on it when you are at work and then call back. Make sure that it says, "Jim's Antiques, home of professionally selected merchandise. We are sorry that we are away making a delivery right now, but if you leave your name and number ..." and not "Mary and I are not in right now ...."

One final point on yellow pages:

Have you ever noticed that some of the advertisements have the phone number in big, bold numbers, with no address shown?

Why do you suppose this is?

"You want to visit with them rather then get a letter."

Ten out of ten, professional. Yes, you want to talk with them. It builds rapport.

Newspaper advertising. Lots of antique dealers do this. I don't. Certainly not in the daily papers.

"In antique papers?"

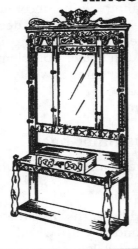

KINGS ANTIQUES

Come to **Kings Antiques** to find exquisite pieces like this circa 1880 hall tree from England. It has heavy, old mellow oak with turned finials and has the original metal drip-pano with handles. Note the sea horse carvings, they were very popular during this period. Picture this imposing piece at the entrance of your home! Each detail is elaborately carved in this rich oak hall stand that has turned wood hanging pegs. The original bevelled mirror is intact. This is just one example of the specially hand picked pieces that you'll find at **Kings Antiques**. Mon-Sat. 10-6. 316 S. Main, Grapevine. 329-0760.

Newspaper advertising. Lots of antique dealers do this.

Yes, definitely.

"Why don't you like daily papers?"

I don't like the scattergun approach in anything I do. The interior decorating and antique business is like deep sea fishing. If you want to catch a big marlin, don't bait a lot of tiny hooks with sardines. Bait your man-sized triple hook with a ten-pound tuna. Add a couple more hooks down the side of the tuna's body and ... bingo! One proud photograph to take home.

Use specialized bait for specialized customers. That word "special" keeps cropping up, doesn't it?

Having said all that, daily newspaper advertising works for some, but since you are a growing dealer (the word growing sounds better than small, doesn't it?), target any advertising you do. It gives more bang for your money.

Flyers. I'm a great believer in these. They are targeted, specific, bold, and quite often cheap. I have a very special deal with a good company. They design the flyer to my suggestion, print it, and mail-drop it for me. Based on my customer base areas, they do 13,000 flyers for me for as little as $300. Is that a good deal, or what?

You can get the same, if you fight hard for it. Check around, look for the cheap coupon companies. Ask them to do a flyer for you and insert it in their coupon books. No, not in a coupon form, in a flyer form. Just like my sample in the illustration on page 138.

"But if I put it in a cheap coupon book, people will think that I sell cheap merchandise. You told me to go high-end in my booth."

Wrong! People think it just got stuck in the coupon book because it's full-sized and overhangs the edges. It's all perception. How can the flyer come with the coupons if it's not the same size? That's not possible. Jim's Antiques, Home of Professionally Selected Merchandise, must have sent it to me especially and it just got messed up in the mail.

One final thing. Notice how little detail there is on the flyer. Lots of information, but little detail. Did you know that most people only have an attention span of ten seconds? If you haven't hooked them by then, you've lost them. Big, bold, and clear gets them every time!

Flyers are good. Customers stick them on the refrigerator door and two months later call in. Tons of detail and they throw it out with the fish heads. Yuk!

Flyers. I'm a great believer in these.

Follow up by phone

If you check your customer register and someone writes nice things, call and thank them. Also send the card. Build your customer base by projecting your very special personality. Appear caring.

I always remember how surprised I was when I first came to America and people called me by my first name. It seemed very rude and overly familiar. I soon got to like it. In England if you did it, it would be considered pushy and presumptuous. My wonderful English friends are warm, but very reserved.

I prefer the American way. It helps break down the barriers. The same goes for the telephone in building your essential customer base. Use it to the max.

Chapter 11 review

1. Carry suitable products for your customers and make a big fuss over them to **build a large customer base as quickly as possible**.

2. **Network with other dealers** to develop new customers.

3. **Use discount coupons for your special customers only**. Ask them to pass one on to their friends as a special thank you to them.

4. **Make the camera an essential sales tool**. Take photos to ensure you get the piece you bought and use them to pre-sell it.

5. **Interior decorators can be a great help** when building a customer base. Make sure that all conditions are upfront and understood so that neither of you get embarrassed.

6. **Yellow pages, newspaper ads, and flyers** are all good advertising. Flyers are best. Use them to the max.

7. **Use the telephone**. Follow up and it will pay hand-over-fist in increasing customer satisfaction.

$ $ $ $ $

The larger your customer base, the more sales you will make and the more money goes into the bank. That's a part we haven't covered yet. I've enjoyed it so far. Hope you have.

In the next chapter we cover monthly operations, which can get quite complex. In all you do, however, remember that the more customers that come into your booth, the more money will go through your till.

12. Monthly Operations

"What a professionally run booth. Every month they have something new!" said the little old dear to her companion.

Those are the words you want to hear when standing quietly beside your booth eavesdropping on the passing traffic.

Eavesdropping is the best, cheapest, and most accurate way of finding out what the buying public thinks of your operation. If you're good, you'll hear the words, "They've always got something new" peppering the conversations. You might also hear very unflattering things, but if you can't take the heat during critique sessions, you shouldn't be in the kitchen. You should be in a Tibetan monastery in the Himalayas!

To keep the buying public's interest high, we have to change out our booth every month at least. We also have to do it every time we sell a piece of furniture.

Changing out your booth every month makes old merchandise look new. I am always surprised at how well this works. Even customers that come in regularly will say, "That's new. I haven't seen that before." Little can they remember that the same porcelain vase was staring them in the face during their last three visits while I stood by wishing that they'd take it home with them. Okay, so I have put a flower arrangement in it to bring out the pink and blues in the design, but it's still the same vase, isn't it?

Not only should you change the merchandise, but you should also change the arrangement. Instead of having the new sideboard angled in the corner just like you had the halltree, you should put it in the opposite corner.

Keep experimenting. Try anything, even if it looks a little way out. Everyone's different and you never know how people will react. Just by shuffling the furniture and accessories around, you will make it look like new inventory. The light will catch your accessories from a different angle and they will trigger a different response from your customers.

I always remember a porcelain conch vase that my staff positioned on the right side of a dark buffet. It was a beautiful Worcester one with a red rose pattern and sat there for two months being admired by all. One Friday I changed it around and put it on the left side where some overhead spotlights highlighted it. About ten minutes later a lady who had seen it many times before came in. "How gorgeous!" she exclaimed and reached for her checkbook.

Why? Because it had a whole different look. Same piece, just a different look. As she walked out clutching the parcel, I overheard her saying to her friend, "I can put it on the left side where the sunlight from the window will catch it." Go figure it. Just remember that most of us have to work at being imaginative, so we want to see a piece as it would look in our room, and expect it to be displayed as such.

So ... do the monthly shuffle.

It's necessary, it sells more, and it makes your booth look like a winner. Even if you don't have any new merchandise, shuffle around what you have in your booth. It gives you something to do on that Sunday evening.

Changing color

Changing color is the next best thing to shuffling around. I know you're not a painter; you don't have to be. When I talk of changing color I don't mean repainting the whole booth. Even I wouldn't do that. What I mean is paint a small side wall with a contrasting color to change the overall look. Repainting trim does the same thing, although I personally hate all the masking required.

My best advice is that you get yourself a plan of action. This month you will paint the two side walls peach to go with the green, and sixty days from now you will paint the trim, and so on.

I know it sounds like a lot of work, but it does give it a fresh look and helps sales.

Themes

One of the most effective ways of getting that new look is to use themes. The dictionary defines theme as "an idea, point of view, or perception embodied and expanded upon in a work of art." Taking this literally, all you have to do is to expand on the painted wall (work of art) that you did.

"Sure," I hear you say, "I had enough trouble just painting the flat wall, and that's no work of art!"

How about this then?

This month you are changing out and putting in a bedroom setting. You bought the French oak bed together with its matching bedside tables and amoire. It all looks great against the dark green and peach colored paint scheme. Now here's the kicker!

Go to your local wallpaper store and purchase wallpaper border with a cat theme. Put it up all around the top of your booth. Chuck some tapestry pillows with a cat pattern on the bed and hang a few cat patterned throws around. Add the antique Dutch porcelain cats that you had in the back of your garage and hang two cat pictures on the wall. Bingo! See what I mean? And it didn't take too long. Moving the furniture in took the longest, about forty-five minutes. Sticking the self-adhesive cat theme border took another thirty, and the rest? … about thirty minutes more. All together, including the coke break, it took about two hours.

Monthly promotions

While doing all this shuffling, painting, wallpapering, and throwing cat pillows on the bed, pick one piece. Write a nice sign saying:

Special Buy!

Nice French marble-topped bedside table. One of four
bought at a special price. In appreciation of your business, we are passing the savings on to you and this fine
furniture accent piece is priced at a low $395.00 for this
month only.

Note I didn't say "normally $595. Special price $395." I hate
those. Everyone knows that they are a lie. Even worse is the one
that goes, "Sale! sale! sale! Was $595, $495, now $395." Every time
I see those tags I want to ask the dealer, "Does nobody want it?"

Be proud of your merchandise and act like a professional
antique dealer and not like a suave, commissioned salesman.

Enough on promotions.

Paperwork!

There's that ugly word again. Don't worry, this time I'm not
going to talk about accounts. The paperwork I'm talking about
in your monthly operations is the upkeep of your price tags.
These are the ones with the interesting story that you wrote
about each piece and on which you have your asking price.
After all the handling, they become tatty. Rewrite them if
necessary—it gives a good impression. Everyone loves a
winner and if your price tags become worn, your customers
will get the feeling that you don't care.

Planning ahead

"So much to remember! With all the above, how am I ever
going to remember it all every month?"

By making a list.

So what do we have to remember every month?

1. Change everything around.
2. Paint. Use color to give your booth a new look.
3. Occasionally use border wallpaper to build a theme.
   This is excellent when combined with a particular
   range of products. You can do this because you are an
   interior accessory and antique professional.

4. Mark one piece of furniture as a special promotion to thank your loyal customers. They'll look out for it every time they come in.

5. Make a new list every month. If you can, do it in the middle of the month so that you can start thinking about it early—it'll help you at the auctions and garage sales, and when perusing the antique section of the newspaper. You can start buying those small accessories to fit in with next month's setting.

It doesn't take much to think ahead and be prepared. It will pay you dividends in extra sales!

Day to day regime

I've left this section for last in this chapter for a reason. That reason is that having pushed, badgered, and cajoled you to work, work, and work some more, it's time to tell you also to relax and have fun. To help you make money and enjoy doing it, I will suggest a weekly schedule for you. Change it, keep it flexible, and use it as a guide only. The point is, plan ahead.

Before I go into it, however, I would like to take this opportunity to tell you about my experience as an international pilot. You didn't know that I was an international jet pilot as well as an antique dealer? Sorry, it must have slipped my mind. Anyway, here's the story:

When I first got promoted to flying international routes out of Nairobi, Kenya, I thought that I would never master the approach routes into Rome, Paris, and London. Can you imagine how frightening it is to suddenly be thrust out of the empty skies over Africa and fly into the most densely populated airspace in the world?

To add to this, the Italian air traffic controllers spoke English with funny guttural accents and I could hardly understand them. By the time I wrote Chivetivechio (Chi-ve-ti-ve-chi-ow) on my approach pad, we were past it and the captain was yelling at me to tell him what the next checkpoint was! Not only did I not know, but even if I had, I would not have been able to pronounce it!

Finally I decided to take matters into my own hands. During a day off, I went to Rome Fumacino airport and visited with the controllers during their rest break. As with most high pressure jobs, they worked two hours on and two hours off. Being so hyper, they were bored after one hour of rest and were more than willing to help me overcome my problem. This is what they told me:

"Nothing is random. Everything is planned. With this in mind, all aircraft coming into our airspace from the south, such as Africa and Arabia, have to follow the route over Chivetivechio, Ostia, and Ponza."

Once I knew this, my problem was solved.

I didn't have to hear the words exactly, all I had to do was to catch the first syllable and I was home and dry!

Soon I was even able to look out of the window in between checkpoints. Since I knew what to expect, I was no longer flustered by the unknown and was able to confidently anticipate the next designated checkpoint—where it was, and even how my Italian friends pronounced it.

It's the same with running your antique business. Once you get into a comfortable routine, you will be able to relax and enjoy it.

Here is what I suggest you follow:

Monday: Watch Monday night football. It's usually a quiet day.

Tuesday: Go to the mall on your way home from work, or when you have time. Nose around, check on what's been going on, and start to think about the weekend's anticipated business. Don't stay too long unless you have to.

Wednesday: Go to your booth and tidy up. Dust and adjust everything to look professional. Check your tags, replace any scruffy looking ones. Talk to the mall owner and ask about business in general. Listen; don't talk. If a booth is doing particularly well, go visit it and find out why.

Thursday: Watch TV.

Friday: Take a loved one out to dinner. Don't talk antiques.

Saturday: Go to your booth at 11 a.m. Be a fine host. Talk to customers and other dealers, and sell your heart out. This is your big day. Work it to the max. Stay as long as necessary but take a break occasionally. The busy periods are around 11 a.m. and 4 p.m. Be there.

Sunday: Most malls open between 12 noon and 5 p.m. Visit during this time to tidy up after Saturday and restock if necessary. Once a month, shuffle everything after 5 p.m. If everything's under control, don't stick around and get bored. Go home, but only if your booth is set for another week.

The point here is, don't work yourself to death. It's supposed to be fun. With a plan, everything becomes easier, just like flying into Rome. You can take down those accessories on Tuesday and not on Saturday when customers are milling about. Once a month, don't go to the mall on Tuesday; do your books instead. Saturday is always for selling—if you have to take down that huge wardrobe, do it on Tuesday. Other dealers will definitely not appreciate you blocking the aisle with your clumsy furniture on Saturday afternoon. They might even give you a hand on Tuesday.

Anticipate with planning. Business will become so much more enjoyable for you and everybody else. Make up a schedule that suits you best and have fun because you are in charge. You are driving the business, not vice versa.

I have one other suggestion:

If you are like me, there will be days when you will be bored. Nothing's going on and the mall is quiet. You've already dusted everything at least twice and your irritation level is rising. You want to feel as if you have done something constructive, but you just can't think of what else to do.

Go visit other malls outside your immediate area.

I always take my little recorder with me when I do this. If I see something new or interesting, I record my impressions for future use. It's amazing how much you can learn from others and how this will make your black mood disappear. As I have said before, no one has a monopoly on knowledge.

Chapter 12 review

1. **Shuffle monthly**. It's a must.

2. **Become a part-time painter** occasionally. Someone will appreciate it.

3. How about cats, dogs, rabbits, roses, lace, etc., for a **theme**?

4. A special piece "just for you" will **make your customers feel wanted and loved**.

5. Make sure that those **tags look fresh**, not tatty and tired.

6. **Plan next month's shuffle**. It will give you time to find that extra salable merchandise.

7. **Set yourself a comfortable routine**. Have fun as well as make money.

$ $ $ $

In all the previous chapters we have covered the **basics** of making you successful. In the next chapters we will start fine tuning. I find it one of the most interesting aspects of the business. I think you will too. Let's do it!

13. Extra Ways to Boost Income

I'm looking forward to covering this with you. It will give you a real edge because most dealers don't even know how to calculate their income, let alone boost it. They get so bogged down in the day-to-day running of their business, that they don't see the forest for the trees. Now I know that what I'm going to suggest will not be for everyone, but for those who want to succeed, the extra ways to boost income will come as a pleasant surprise. Some of it I have already covered briefly and so I will start with that.

Using other dealers

If you remember, I have already advised you that you should get to know your neighboring dealers. Having done this, you should consider combining your buying and selling, especially with regard to a particular range of products. For example, by placing your crystal vase among your friend's larger grouping, it is likely to sell quicker. In turn, he or she can let you sell those two porcelain bedside lamps in your booth, since you specialize in lamps. Allocate each other a small commission and you will both gain.

By cooperating, you both have larger retail space without extra overhead.

Now, how about taking this one step further?

The best way to explain this is with an example: Near my store there is a well-run antique mall. Four of the dealers have formed a co-op. Working with one of the dealers, I put some of my better pieces of furniture into her booth. This enables her to change out more often. She, in turn, puts lamps into my store. Working closely, we direct customers to each other for a particular requirement. The twenty percent commission we allocate against the sale enables us both to gain. Believe me, the extra retail space without extra overhead helps boost the bottom line.

Why don't you do the same with dealers in nearby locations? It works well. You'll be amazed how many new friendships you can develop this way and it adds fun to the business while increasing your sales at the same time.

How to find special customers to boost income

What does "special customer" mean to you? Does it mean friendly, extra nice, fun to be with? Maybe all of those things. But special customers also mean special profits.

Where do we find these special customers to make these special profits? By looking outside the mainstream of the antique business. How about the local women's business association? Or the women's chapter of the Chamber of Commerce? Or the local Readers Club? There is usually one in your town. They are all a great source of new customers.

"I can see that, but how do I attract them to my booth?"

Just think of this: If you could arrange to give them a talk on antiques at their next meeting, and while doing this, give each of them a special invitation and discount card, you would have tapped into a whole group of special customers at one time. How about that as a thought?

Of course, they'll want you to join their associations! But so what? You'll have the inside track to their business and the profits from the extra sales will more than cover the cost of memberships.

Special customers are those other than the ones who normally come into the mall and visit your booth. It's like commercial fishing. Spread your net far and wide and you will have a better chance of a good catch!

Restaurants—wonderful special customers

I can see your eyes light up. You remembered the tables and chairs I talked about in an earlier chapter. You are getting good.

When you next go into a restaurant, particularly those privately owned ones, look around. What do you see? Decor. And what makes the decor different? Pictures, subdued lighting, wall decorations, and furniture all play their part. Even the large restaurant chains are now using antiques to give that certain ambiance. If you don't believe me, just look around. I guarantee you will see old golf clubs, milk cans, old dog carts, pictures, saddles, musical instruments, and many, many more antiques decorating the place.

Restaurants are excellent special customers. Not only have I sold accessories to them, but I have also supplied large numbers of draw-leaf tables and chairs, as well as buffets and pictures. Being commercial operations, they usually purchase quantity and therefore give your normal sales a real boost. If you can develop a good relationship with the owner, he or she will very often use you as a consultant. After all, we all want someone's expertise for free, don't we? And you don't mind giving it. You'll make it up on the sales. It might even get you the reputation of being the expert to contact. Word of mouth is great advertising.

"And it's free!"

So you were taking note. That makes me feel good.

But a word of warning. Back in Chapter 1, I mentioned staying cool. Remember that? I have also told you about the restaurant that messed around with me by getting a price on tables and chairs, and then cut the order down. "If it stinks, don't step in it," is my motto for those situations.

Remember that motto when dealing with restaurants. Particularly the private ones, but it applies to all equally. Restaurant owners are notorious for starting their businesses on a shoestring and hoping that cash flow will carry them through. Make sure you get a deposit. Don't, don't, don't take the order without one. If you do, you're liable to have spent your money buying all the decorative pieces or furniture and having no customer. Worse still, you may end up not being paid. While you are about it, make sure that the deposit covers your costs. Thirty to fifty percent is usual.

"How do we find these restaurants?"

A. Go to your local chamber of commerce and ask!
B. When having dinner at another restaurant, casually ask the owner if there are any new ones being planned, his or others.
C. Keep your ears open and you will be surprised how much you hear.
D. When traveling to garage sales, keep your eyes open and watch for those banners proclaiming "Opening soon - Georgio's Italian Ristorante." In particular, look in the strip malls. That's where they usually are.
E. Stop by your local planning/permit office. They will have plans for any proposed eating houses going up. This way, you will be the early bird in finding out their decorative requirements.

In closing this section I would urge you to take the time and trouble to contact restaurants. They are good business. Stay cool, get deposits, and you can't go wrong.

Banks, lawyers' offices, doctors' offices, etc.

Professional offices like to project a classy impression. Nothing does this better than beautiful antique furniture. Lawyers in particular like large antique bookcases for their numerous reference books. So do doctors. Banks like fancy, ornate buffets or writing desks for their customers to use. I suggest you offer the following furniture pieces:

For lawyers and doctors: antique desks, bookcases, magazine tables, antique clocks, and pictures.

For banks and other professional offices: antique desks, magazine tables, statues, and pictures.

"Isn't that a lot of effort? I've got more than enough work to do already," I hear you complaining.

Yes, it is, but while you are doing your paperwork, get your partner in your now-thriving business to take out the yellow pages and list all the lawyers' and doctors' names and addresses. Write a cover letter and photocopy it. Hand write in the names and addresses and attach your flyer to each one before mailing.

In closing, I would like to recommend that you always keep an open mind. Antiques are used everywhere. You can never put in enough effort in developing business with special customers.

Collectibles are the hot thing! More and more people collect Depression glass, Flow Blue plates, etc.

Not only do they buy antiques for their offices, but also for their homes. Their friends do too.

Collectible associations

Collectibles are the hot thing. More and more people are collecting Flow Blue plates, perfume bottles, Depression glass, Dresden porcelain, and many other items. Although I told you earlier that I recommend avoiding collectibles, I should have clarified it.

I still believe that avoiding collectibles is the best policy when starting out, but you are now an expert. Since your business is up and running, you can now find out more about a particular collectible that interests you. Whatever it is, look up the address of the association specializing in it. There is bound to be one. Most have large memberships and regular newsletters and many even hold biannual conferences.

"How does all this help me boost my income?"

Join and become a member. On your buying trips to the auction, garage sales, estate sales, and even in your contacts with private sellers, watch out for your collectible pieces. By advertising in the association's newsletter, you have a captive group of buyers and are not relying just on walk-in traffic. Now it's worth bothering with collectibles because you can sell your items relatively quickly. Don't forget, every bit helps. All you have to do is the extra work.

Antique shows

In the *Antique Traveller* newspaper you will find the dates of all the national antique shows. There is bound to be one near you. Since they are heavily advertised by their promoters, they draw large crowds and I would recommend that you try to show at as many as you can. Take a register with you that visitors to your booth can fill in. By using this, together with the one in your booth, you have an instant mailing list to which you can mail flyers. This is a particularly good way of boosting income.

Mailing lists

In the above section I mention using a mailing list. The names gathered at the antique shows, plus the customers filling in the visitor's book at your booth, will give you the basis of a good mailing list. You can enlarge on this by buying names from your local mailing list company. For those of you who don't know, these companies can supply names based on income level, residential area, and even personal preferences. My suggestion is that you purchase the minimum number of names every time you have a decent cash flow situation. Doing it this way minimizes the financial outlay and continues to build up your direct mailing list over a period of time.

"But it costs too much to send out letters at thirty-two cents a copy, and isn't the cost of printing prohibitive?"

Yes, but here are some suggestions to keep the cost down:

1. Buy a bulk mailing permit. This will enable you to mail at a cheaper rate. There are quantity and sorting requirements, so check with your local post office.
2. Instead of printing letters, use the flyers that your coupon stuffing company does for you. If you are clever, you'll ask them to print a few hundred extra for you every time they do a flyer for you. My coupon company actually gives me about one hundred copies whenever I do a mail drop with them. Over a period of time I collect about five hundred free flyers, which enables me to do a direct mailing of my own.

It is the norm in the gift and furniture business to allocate about seven percent of your sales to advertising. The secret is to ensure that this outlay is utilized on the most effective form of advertising. In my case, the flyer mail drop coupled with the occasional direct mailing gives me the best results. Try it for yourself and see.

$ $ $ $ $

Well, did you have fun? Can you see how you can boost your normal sales by doing a little extra work in the evenings? Isn't it exciting that the market for antiques is not just restricted to walk-in customers, but reaches into professional offices as well? Take advantage of it. It's an exciting business!

The purpose of this chapter was not just to show what else you can do to earn extra income, but to get you started on thinking that there is a market for your antiques in the most unlikely places. If I have been able to do that, then I will have achieved my objective.

Chapter 13 review

1. **Network with other dealers** to form a co-op specializing in more than one product line in addition to your normal business. It draws the customers to you first.

2. **Look for markets outside the antique mainstream**. Local women's associations, readers clubs, and the chamber of commerce are all fertile ground. Offer to be a guest speaker at their next luncheon meeting.

3. Selling draw-leaf tables and buffets to **restaurants** is a fantastic way to boost income. Just remember, "If it stinks, don't step in it," or ask for a larger deposit. This really takes you into the wholesale business in a big way.

4. **Lawyers' offices, doctors' offices, banks, and almost any professional office** need dignified antique furniture to project a classy impression. Reach out and sell to them.

5. **Collectible associations** open a captive audience. Use them.

6. **Antique shows** build your mailing list, which boosts your income while only slightly increasing overhead.

7. **Use the mailing list**. Get free extra copies of your flyer and increase your direct mailing list by purchasing additional names from your local business names company.

$$ \$\ \$\ \$\ \$\ \$ $$

"Is all this extra work worth it?"

Yes. I wouldn't be telling you about it if it wasn't, would I? But don't try to do it all at once. Start with restaurants, lawyers' offices, and doctors first, and then feed the rest in slowly. If you're not careful you'll soon need a secretary.

You think I'm joking?

Wait till you read the next chapter.

14. Expanding

Expansion!

Have we really got this far? Wow! Only a short time ago we were talking about "is it for you?" and "getting started," and now here we are talking about expanding your business. That's what happens when you are determined and apply the ability you have.

Expansion—how to do it, and what problems you are likely to encounter—is our subject.

First of all, when should you start to expand from one booth to more than one? I believe that the answer to that lies in a number of factors and not in just one. It is an exciting period when you reach this stage of your business and you should apply as much thought to it as you did in starting. Let's ask ourselves some questions:

1. Do you like the business?	Yes	Unsure
2. Are you still finding it exciting?	Yes	No
3. Is it still interesting or do you do it just for the money?	Yes	Money
4. Have you coped reasonably with the stresses?	Yes	No

5. Has your partner enjoyed it?	Yes	No
6. Does he/she want to continue?	Yes	No
7. Have you made money?	Yes	No
8. Enough to expand and possibly inject more of your own money into it?	Yes	No
9. Do you have more to invest?	Yes	No
10. Without it bankrupting you?	Yes	No
11. Are you prepared to put in more time to run a larger business?	Yes	No
12. Do you think the fun will still be in it if you do?	Yes	Maybe
13. Are you much more confident about your ability to buy and sell right?	Yes	No
14. Have you made new friends?	Yes	No
15. Have you had fun?	Yes	Sometimes
16. Do you want to expand?	Yes	Unsure

If the majority of your answers are yes, go for it! If there are some that seriously worry you—I mean seriously worry you and not just leave you unsure—then reconsider. If you have three or more serious reservations, I recommend that you put any expansion plans on hold. Come back to them at a later date.

But if you don't, GO FOR IT!

Coping with success

What a terrific thought!

Coping with success requires you to follow all the same basic steps that we covered in starting, only more so. Can you remember that far back? Seems a long time ago, doesn't it?

So what was the first thing that I recommended?

"Slow down! Cool it."

You do remember. Well done. Why did I recommend that?

"Because more mistakes are made and more money lost in the initial surge of excitement than you cared to remember!"

That's right. Why do I recommend the same again when expanding?

"Because this time around I could lose even more!"

Exactly! Not only could you lose more money, but you could also lose the very nice business that you've built up.

So we are going to act very, very cool and make intelligent, professional decisions. Almost like being part of corporate America, isn't it? Read on.

How to expand

The most important decision you will make in growing your business is how and what direction you are going to take. It may sound easy, but it's not.

"Why? All I have to do is to rent another booth."

Wrong. You are going to have to put a lot more thought and research into it than that, and the first question you are going to have to ask yourself is, "Is this the only way?"

Of course not. So let's discuss your options:

1. **Is it best to open another booth in the same mall?**
2. **Should I open it in a nearby mall?**
3. **Is this the only way?**
4. **If it isn't, what other way of expanding is there?**
5. **Am I going to do it on my own, or is it better to do it with friends who are also thinking of expanding?**

To help you make your own decision, I offer you the following alternatives. Think long and hard over this, because in the end you are on your own. Only you can make the decision. Good luck.

Is it best to open another booth in the same mall?

How have you done? If you have made good money in your present location it might be worth staying where you are. There are some things to consider, however:

1. Are you happy with the way the mall is run?

2. Do you think business will keep increasing or is there a new mall drawing off some of the customers?

3. Can you get another booth next to your present one, or two together in an equally good position? Don't forget that a larger space made up of two units will always attract more customers than two separate ones. You

can also do more with it (i.e. arrange a dining room and a living room setting together instead of just one or the other).

4. Will the owner give you a discount for renting more space? Press for it, and if he or she won't, you might be better off in the new mall.

Here I will give you a most important piece of advice. Bear it in mind at all times. It will be the key ingredient in your success.

When expanding, keep your overhead down, down, down! Do not double it just because you are doubling your business. Profits do not rise proportionately to your overhead, which always rises out of whack.

A new motto might help here: "I like traveling first class and don't intend to go back to tourist."

In deciding to stay in the same mall, consider whether you can keep increasing business, keep your overhead down, and if you are happy with the way things are run. Getting the two or three booths together should also influence your decision. Some of my experience might help you here.

Do you remember me mentioning the booth Beverly and I took in a nearby mall? Yes, the one where I did so well in the first month! I have to make the same decision as you do on expanding in this mall. A little background is in order here.

When we took the booth, the mall had just opened. It was the second location to be opened by the same owners and their first one has a great reputation. This second one, however, has not done as well as the original. It is divided into crafts and antiques and it's obvious that the craft side is doing great, while the antique side is slow. All the craft booths are let, while only half the antique ones are.

Watching the customer traffic over a long period, I have noticed that most visitors are buying very low priced knickknacks.

What does that tell you?

"That the customer base is a working class type, not a professional office type. They buy lower priced merchandise, not higher priced antiques; more cute stuff than home accessories."

Excellent! A perfect observation. What would be your decision be if you were us?

"Move to another location. You can't afford to wait in the hope that the customer base will change."

First class! I can see that you are more than capable of making coldly logical decisions on your expansion plans.

Opening in a nearby mall

Some dealers will tell you that this is a better bet because you are not putting all your eggs in the same basket. I don't subscribe to that theory because I'm not in the egg business. You, like me, are in the money business first, and in the interior decorating and antique business second. The egg business doesn't even figure.

Spreading yourself usually increases overhead. You certainly won't get a discount on just one new booth in the other mall. It will also take more time to look after two booths in different locations. Your gas bill will go up, and you will certainly miss those Sunday afternoon football games traveling between the two locations.

The only reason for spreading yourself between two malls is if you think that another mall could be a better bet in drawing more customers, or if you are not happy with the way your mall is run. Depending on the other location, it could also draw a different caliber of customer. One with more money to spend due to it being in a higher income area? If so, consider it seriously. Otherwise, forget it!

So … these are my recommendations:

1. Get another booth in the same mall if business is good and you are happy with the management.

2. If you have doubts on the above, get a new booth in a different location.

3. Consider this anyway if the customer base in the new location is of a higher income level.

Just don't forget: Keep those increasing expenses down! Do one trip between booths, not two. That means get organized. Visit one booth one day, and the second on another day.

There is another excellent alternative, which I highly recommend if you are considering expanding. It needs organizing, but is the best and most effective way of expanding your antique business.

Opening your own place with other dealers

Remember when we discussed getting your co-op going in that corner of the mall where you and your friends banded together so as not to compete in the same product lines? Does it work well for you? Do you all get on with each other? Yes? ... Great!

How about the four or five of you expanding together then?

This is the single most effective way of expanding while keeping your overhead down. It will increase the value of all your businesses, help you keep down the hours you will have to work, and give you the muscle to get discounts on products and services. Not only will you draw new customers, you will also stamp your own mark on the business and stand out as a professionally run operation. And that's not the best part.

You can still have your own individual businesses, only now you will split all the overhead. This becomes much more economical.

Just think of it like this: If four of you each take another booth in the mall you are in, it will cost a total of $2000 in rent (two times $250 each, times the four of you). Even if the mall owner gives you a discount, it will still cost you about $1800.

By renting a commercially zoned house, you should not pay more than $1400 per month. Try to get a house. (Retail space will do in a pinch, but it's not as full of character and you will have to spend money on the interior to get the cozy ambiance you want in the antique business.) Not only will it be cheaper in a house, but it will certainly double your individual space. After all, eight booths total eight hundred square feet. The house will be at least fifteen hundred, if not eighteen hundred, square feet. And yes, you can use every room, including the bathroom, to display products for sale. Not only that, just think of how you can all decorate it. You will be the biggest draw in the area!

"That sounds like fun!"

Yes. It can be. Let's run with the idea further.

Think of how much more leeway you will all have in attracting customers and therefore increasing sales. Promotions, open days, special Christmas events, the list is endless. But most of all, you and your friends' businesses will have developed your own personality for your own SPECIAL customers. They will no longer feel that your booth is terrific but only a part of another entity. Now you can really go to town in giving them the service they expect. Just think, you can have coffee and cookies at the door, offer delivery (for which you charge), and even have wine and cheese parties for your best customers.

The wine and cheese parties are what really makes customers feel special. I always hold these, by special invitation only, whenever I get new inventory in.

"What's the downside?"

You already know it: organization. You will no longer have the mall owners to take in payments, pay the taxes, and look after the place.

"No big deal."

Not as long as you are organized, get on with each other, and all pull your weight. Of these three, the second is the most important. If there is even a shadow of a doubt about anyone, don't invite him/her to join your co-op. Invite someone else.

"How do we organize ourselves?"

The best way for me to answer that question is to use a co-op I know as an example, namely my friends at Village Treasures in Grapevine.

The first thing they did was arrange a work schedule to suit everybody, while covering a seven-day-a-week operation. In allocating the times and days they would each work, it became obvious that some could put in more hours than others. In exchange, the partners that couldn't be there as often were allocated the bookkeeping and paperwork chores. Others took up the slack and one partner was designated the decorating of the windows every month. In this way, the staffing and paperwork are taken care of.

Since they are all independent but connected, all incoming shipments are handled by the person on duty and everyone helps out in loading and packing. Checks for UPS are kept in a drawer so that incoming shipments are received as soon as possible.

All costs and overhead of the group are split absolutely evenly. There is no deviation from this.

Finally, they do something that I think is essential. Once a month, they have a co-op meeting to discuss everything, sort out any differences, and cover future planning. They also have a fabulous dinner after the meeting.

It works great for them. So great in fact, that they also have an occasional girls' night out, and as another excuse to drink margaritas or Texas Teas, they celebrate each other's birthdays.

Their standing joke is, "Whose birthday is it this month?" If there isn't one, they make one up.

I recommend that you find the right co-op partners to expand, if you can. It is the best, the cheapest, and the safest way to grow your business. Not only that, sometime in the future you may all want to open another branch and decide to incorporate as a company in which you will all have an equal shareholding.

There is one final thing I would do if I were them. I would draw up a simple letter of agreement covering all salient points and recommend that they each sign it. I don't know if they have done this because I am not that nosy. Arrogant and big-headed I might be, but not nosy. I can hear the chuckles from Village Treasures even now!

Since I recommend this way of growing your business if possible, I will highlight its advantages and disadvantages.

Advantages

More retail space for less rent.

You can develop your own business character.

You will all be able to treat customers royally.

You share overhead, therefore less risk.

You share working hours.

If you can get a house rather than retail space, all your businesses will benefit from the extra wall space, storage space, and unique character.

The co-op can become an incorporated business if growth continues.

Once a month you have a terrific evening out at the co-op's expense. Just don't drink too much and get testy. Cheerful yes, testy no! Don't forget, you have to work with your co-op partners the next day.

Disadvantages

You must all get along together.

Everyone must pull their own weight and if someone doesn't, you will have to advise them to pull their socks up. This can be awkward.

It's difficult to get individual insurance coverage with no central owner.

You will all have to sign the lease jointly and it is likely to be for at least a year. This means a long-term commitment.

If you can expand your business in this way—do it! It's a fabulous way of making more money and having fun. The advantages are numerous and the disadvantages few. The key is personalities. If everyone in your group gets along, go for it.

Finding expansion money

This is an important subject in any business, more so in the antique business be-cause banks and loan depart-ments always prefer new merchandise as collateral. Try explaining that any antique is new merchandise in its own right because that's what the customer is looking for, and you are liable to get a very strange look from the bank manager.

A few minutes later I sold a very nice 1880 French dresser to a customer in Little Rock, Arkansas.

So how do you find expansion money?

1. By injecting more of your own.

2. By building credit worthiness with other dealers. Give them a two week post-dated check for merchandise if they trust you. The piece might just sell before the check is due.

3. By increasing the purchases of replica lamps, repro-duction pictures, rugs, and antique-looking pillows. Get them on thirty day account. (It's all money. You are an interior decorating and antique business remem-

ber?) Just don't buy reproduction furniture unless you are very, very sure of what you are doing.

4. By taking in more consignments. Now that you have a system set up, there's no problem. Consignments will increase your cash flow without any outlay of capital.

I must tell you a story about this, that I just heard today. An interior decorator came into my store this afternoon and asked me if I knew of a large antique dealer who had gone out of business about ten months ago. The decorator had done business with them. In our conversation she said this:

"They were great to buy from until they started loading their inventory with consignment reproductions. I asked them why they had changed and they told me that it had gotten more difficult to get good genuine antiques. Unfortunately, my clients saw the same repro pieces around the corner and pestered me to buy them there because they were cheaper, or else stopped dealing with me altogether. I wish they had simply put up their prices and stayed with the genuine antique pieces. It would have been better for both of us."

Her words speak for themselves. A few minutes later I sold a very nice 1880 French dresser (see photo) for $1900 to a customer who has a furniture store in Little Rock.

Having said all the above, there is one sure way of financing your expansion plans: **Combine your own extra resources with proper pricing of the merchandise you already have, and you will be able to undertake the steady expansion you desire.**

"You mean plow the profits back into the business, don't you?"

Correct. Price your goods right and it will give you part of your expansion capital.

Chapter 14 review

1. **Have you made enough money and had enough fun to actually want to expand**? Ask yourself the pertinent questions. More importantly, answer them honestly.

2. In coping with your success, **play it cool**. The decisions you now make are as important as the ones you made in getting started and certainly could be far, far more expensive.

3. **How do you expand**? Into another booth in the same mall? Into a new one in a nearby mall? Or best of all, into a house with your co-op friends? There is a lot to think about in all these options. They each have advantages, disadvantages and some may simply not be possible. Read what I have said and then reread it. In this you have to make your own decision. You can do it. You are now very good at the antique business. You know a lot, use your head, and apply yourself.

$$\$\ \$\ \$\ \$$$

Finally, I will close with the expansion motto. You knew one was coming, didn't you?

"I want to keep traveling first class and not go back down to tourist class. In order to do that, I must watch my overhead and keep it down! down! down!"

15. Bits 'n' Pieces

Bits and pieces are part and parcel of the whole antique scene. Many dealers spend too much time and money on them and some dealers spend absolutely no time or money on them.

"What's the best?"

Like always, moderation is best.

Let's take the most talked about "bit 'n' piece" first.

Restoration

Should I do it? Who can I get to do it for me? Should I buy pieces that require it? Is it such a big mystery?

These and a hundred other questions are always asked about restoring antiques. The fact of the matter is that it takes an expert to do it properly and even if you could do it, do you have the gobs of patience that it requires?

Speaking for myself … I do not. Therefore I don't do any restoration and I certainly do not buy anything that requires it. I suggest you avoid it too.

Now I don't mean the cheating kind of restoration.

"Cheating kind?"

Yeah. The kind that only requires a bit of Briwax to hide all the scratches after I've used the oak stain to cover them over. The

British, in particular, are very good at this, and whenever I visit a certain wholesaler in Wales, I am always surprised at the magic that his workshop can do in just a few minutes. It's a funny thing though, in all the restoration work that they have done for me, I have never once seen them strip anything. All they ever do is use the stain, fill in deep grooves with the plastic wax stick, and then polish it with the right colored wax. It makes a one hundred percent difference. For small nicks they use plastic wood, which they stain and polish again.

Here's a tip: Use fine wire wool when waxing, the type you use in your kitchen for scrubbing pots and pans. It smoothes the surface of the wood while also polishing, and the job gets done quickly. Don't use wire wool on a veneer. Only normal household furniture polish does anything on this, and then it only cleans the veneer and gives it a shine. Speaking of veneers, do you know how to repair them when they bubble up?

Veneers are, as everyone knows, wood finishes glued to a base board. They bubble up when the glue gives up its hold. To hold them back down again, get a hot household iron and lay it on a cloth placed over the lifted veneer. It will melt the glue so that the veneer sticks again. If this doesn't do it, go to plan B. Drill a small hole in the center of the bubbled veneer, inject some glue, and repeat the hot iron procedure. Once the glue is dry, fill the drill hole with wood putty, smooth with very fine wire wool, and wax.

The point of the above is time and expertise. You don't have either the time or expertise to do full restoration work. Or do you? Maybe you like fiddling around with such things? In which case, do it and have fun. I far prefer to concentrate on selling, but even if you are like me, take the time and trouble to wax and polish furniture pieces inside and out.

"Inside and out? Is that really necessary? It's all musty smelling!"

Yes. Inside and out. It gives the furniture piece that unusual antique smell and can make the difference between selling it or not. Do it regularly while it's in your booth. With all malls being air-conditioned, the wood tends to dry out, and before you know it you have veneer that is lifting, carved decorations that are falling off, and doors that don't fit. Just imagine the embarrassment when you are selling your heart out to a serious customer and the door of that $4000 armoire won't fit. All the excuses don't help. I know, it's happened to me.

So get yourself a kit together and do the little bit of work necessary to give that furniture piece a shiny, almost new look. Everyone has their favorite products to use. Some like tongue oil, some only household polish. We use Briwax made in England and Fiddes stain, also made in England. Both are available at most large specialist hardware stores. If you can't find them there, check the yellow pages under antique hardware. If you still have trouble getting them, ask around in your mall or drop me a line at Kings in Grapevine, Texas. By the way, I have tried most of the makes out there and the reason I like Briwax is that it comes in different colors. Its most important feature is that it goes on easily and immediately comes off, while doing a great job. No hard rubbing necessary! I don't like hard work.

While I'm on this subject, I may as well cover the wax sticks. These are available in large hardware stores and again come in different wood colors. They work well on deep grooves. All you have to do is melt them with a match and let the melted mixture fill the indent. Let it dry, sand lightly, and presto! ... no groove. Isn't life wonderful?

Talking of wax sticks, when in the hardware store buy yourself a set of stain pens. They come in different wood colors and hide those small scratches with the stroke of a pen! Very useful when delivering furniture. I don't know how often I have loaded a nice item onto the truck to suddenly see an ugly scratch. They seem to come out as soon as you get into the sunlight. A quick stroke of your trusty stain stick and bingo! ... no scratch. Don't forget that furniture is not the only thing that needs touching up. Picture frames, mirror frames, small wooden boxes, and other wooden accessories also need to look their best! Easy when you know how, isn't it?

So here's my ideal antique professional's kit. Put it in a carrying case and use it regularly. It'll keep up the price of your antique furniture, helping it sell quicker.

- 3 tins of Briwax—clear, light brown, and dark brown
- Assortment of wax sticks
- Assortment of stain pens
- Box of matches
- Tin of household polish (for that quick wipe)

- Soft rags
- Small tins of Fiddes stain. Mahogany, oak, and walnut will do.
- Assorted screwdrivers
- Assorted screws
- Assorted grades of wire wool
- Assorted tins of plastic wood
- A selection of assorted picture hangers and picture wire
- Plastic knife (The ones you get at those fast food joints work great.)
- Small hammer
- Utility knife
- Small utility saw (Used to cut that wood block to stop the drawer sliding in! You'll know what I mean when it happens to you.)
- A tube of Wellbond glue (The best I've ever found.)
- A packet of five minute epoxy resin (Sticks those decorations on while you wait!)

Put all the above into an old soft sports bag and you can grab it in a hurry when required. Why is it that those emergency repairs always crop up at awkward moments? Like when the customer's standing there as you are loading up her beautiful buffet?

Different types of wood

The main type of wood used in antiques is oak, with mahogany a close second. Walnut is occasionally seen and cherry is fairly prevalent in American antique furniture. Of them all, mahogany is considered the classy one! It also splits a lot easier. I personally like it because it polishes up beautifully and has a rich lustrous shine.

The best way to learn about these woods is to read up on them in your local library. The rest will come as you become more familiar with them. The main thing you need to know now is that mahogany is dark brown and pricey, walnut is a close second, cherry is usually American, and oak is everywhere. Oak still outsells the rest.

One of the things you will find with English antiques is that they used to stain the oak from a dark brown, almost black in some cases, to a light golden color in other cases. If I was to recommend what to buy, I would recommend that you err on the lighter side. It fits in better with modern decor.

The last wood I would like to discuss is pine. This is immensely popular in England, more so than in the U.S.A. where it is mainly used in dining or breakfast rooms. Because of demand, three types of pine furniture are now available:

Oak still outsells the rest of the woods.

Old pine has dark black knots and cracks in it.

1. Genuine antique pine
2. Modern day manufactured units using old pine retrieved from old buildings
3. New pine furniture stained to look like old pine

"How do I tell which is which?"

Old pine has dark black knots and cracks in it. New pine is almost clean and the wood is almost white. It's quite easy to tell the difference.

Here I must mention a white lie that I hear constantly. If you see a modern manufactured unit and inquire about where the pine came from, you are more than likely to be told "from an old church in England." It's a great sales gimmick but hardly true! There just aren't enough derelict churches in England to supply enough pine for the furniture that is being produced in such masses. Much of it comes from Spain, Portugal, and other places. It still looks good, but is not truly an antique! Having said all that, I like pine.

Here's a tip: The best-selling pine furniture pieces are butcher's blocks, corner curio cabinets, hutches, and farm tables together with chairs and buffets. Wine racks made from old pine also do well.

Here's another tip: Wax pine furniture with clear Briwax. Put lots of it on, the more the better. Let it soak in and then polish. Pine looks absolutely great when this is done—old and very rich!

Finally, I want to talk about glues. The old glues were made from bone, mainly cattle bone. They were very strong, but even so, they will have worn out after fifty odd years! That's why so many antique chairs, tables, buffets, and wardrobes are so rickety. A quick solution to this is to use a modern space-age glue such as Wellbond. Squeeze it into the joints and cracks and it does wonders! The experts will tell you to strip the piece down, clean up the joint and reglue it. That's true for a very special piece, but for my money, I'd rather take the quick fix route, thank you!

Gilt finishes

Gilt finishes are beautiful. True gilt furniture pieces are getting few and far between and the ones I have recently seen are usually French. There is a lot of Far Eastern stuff beginning to flood the market, namely sofas, occasional tables, and mirrors. You can usually tell that it's a reproduction by its shiny, brassy, cheap look. Can you tell that I hate it?

To find if the gilt furniture piece is genuine, check the underside of the wood. If it's old, has old screws, is glued with old glue, and looks weather worn, then it's probably a genuine antique. Many pieces come with marble tops. Gilt finishes were used extensively on entry hall and occasional tables and were

Gilt finishes are beautiful.

combined with marble tops to make them look expensive. You can tell real marble from the artificial resin marble by noting if it's smooth. Real marble has pit holes and cracks, unlike resin marble, which is almost perfectly smooth. You can also tell if it's resin marble by the smell.

"By the smell?"

Yes. Turn the marble over and smell the underside. Polyester resin has a distinct chemical smell. Even when it's old, you can still smell the resin if you scratch it. Just don't do this at the previewing of an auction to check if the top is genuine marble or not. Security will throw you out. That doesn't bother me except that they might send me the bill for telling you to do that!

Once you become an expert you can even tell by feel. Real marble is always cold. Resin is not. Practice! It's the best form of one upmanship if you can put your hand on a marble tabletop and grandly declare, "It's genuine marble!" Of course you have to be right, or else you'll end up with that egg on your face that we discussed earlier on.

To touch up a damaged gilt finish simply go to your nearest well-stocked hardware store. Many carry small glass containers of antique gilt paint. Smear it on with your finger and feather the edges with a fine brush. Once it's dry, dirty your finger slightly, and I mean slightly, and rub the repair. You won't be able to tell where it is unless you know.

Rewiring

Don't buy lamps that require rewiring, unless they're at the flea market or garage sale and the guy is almost paying you to take them away. Then go to your local hardware store and buy all you need. It only takes a half hour and you can do it on that quiet Sunday afternoon when you're bored.

"Why did you tell me not to buy lamps that need rewiring if it's that easy?"

Because if you're like me, you'll end up with a whole pile of them that never get done.

"Does it matter?"

Yes. It matters. It's not businesslike or professional. Think of the money tied up in that lot!

Teapot lids

"Now I know you're off your rocker!"

No, I'm not. It's a very serious subject. It could cost you money.

"What on earth are you talking about?"

Tape down all teapot and other lids with clear, nonresidue office tape. It will save them getting broken and you from getting into an argument with the customer that refuses to pay for it because, "You have insurance, don't you?" Learn from me, all the little things add up.

Delivery

When you first start your business, I would recommend that you do no deliveries whatsoever. It's not necessary and unless you have a truck and want to earn about $30 extra per delivery, it will be more of a nuisance than it's worth. Later on, when you have two or more booths, it might be worth it. The $30 for each delivery adds up and it's good extra spending money if you can do all your deliveries in one day.

If your expansion plans go according to plan and you join your friends in a co-op, then I recommend that you jointly buy a truck and take turns making the deliveries. It becomes part of the necessary service to those special customers.

This reminds me of Rex Fryhover, a man who I consider a friend and who reminds me of myself when I was young. He and I have had a lot of fun making deliveries. It goes without saying that when making deliveries you need two people who are tuned into each other. After all, some of those pieces are heavy! Sometimes, however, tuned into each other is not enough. A large dose of common sense would help, which brings me to something that happened to Rex and me.

We had just picked up a large, massive buffet in Dallas. Carefully positioning it on his pickup, we tied it down well (or so we thought), all the time talking about football. Five minutes later we turned onto the highway and were surprised when cars started honking at us. Rex and I looked at each other, not understanding. Finally we couldn't stand the noise anymore and pulled over. Imagine our surprise to find that we had lost all the elaborately carved drawers on the buffet. They had been flying out one at a time and the cars behind us had been dodging these wooden missiles all the way down the access road.

It could have been expensive! Repairing cars and having a $3500 buffet fixed would have chewed up mucho profit that month, and a few months more besides.

It never happened again. I always check and double check every time we tie something down.

Theft

Theft is part of the business, a horrible part, but a part nonetheless.

Why have I put this subject in here?

Because I want you to realize that it's not worth worrying about if it happens to you. Since it is very difficult to get insurance coverage for your booth in view of it being a public place, the best attitude is

1. To display your goods better, while safeguarding them more. Keeping the smaller pieces in a well lit but locked antique cabinet is one way of protecting yourself. The snag here is that the mall owners must be prepared to keep the key and let a customer see the goods if they ask. In England this is standard practice, but American mall owners have a built-in resistance to doing this for their booth holders. It has something to do with liability. Some new malls have installed a

surveillance camera system and this helps deter crime, but nothing can really stop the experts. They're very good at it.

2. Be philosophical. You've priced in an extra profit and you can't have it always. It is still irritating though!

I want to tell you a story that happened to us in Grapevine. Being a small town, we have a merchant's network. As soon as one of us gets suspicious about a group, we warn all the rest. One day a professional thieves group came into town, and on entering the first store they all split up. The storekeeper couldn't watch them all and by the time she had checked everything and found items missing, they had left her shop. These professional gangs are very good at what they do and never hold onto the stuff. They usually get one member to take it to a "keeper" just outside the area.

Half an hour later, the same gang walked into a picture framing shop. The alert owner tried to watch all five of them and as she was doing so, a sixth member snuck in and made for the cash till. Luckily the owner spotted her and caught her just as her hand dipped into the cash drawer.

Without blinking, the crook looked the owner straight in the eye and said "Let us get out of here without a fuss because we know where you live. You also have a nice store here and sometimes these old shops catch fire because of faulty wiring!"

What would you have done?

I know, you're the macho type like me, right? Just don't be stupid. It's not always worth it.

I told you this to advise you to get angry if something gets stolen, then comfort yourself in the knowledge that you have a reserve built into the price, review how you can minimize theft in the future, and move on. Don't get ulcers over it. It happens!

Insurance

Hard to get for a small business, and if you do, the cost sometimes outweighs the security. Check what kind of policy the mall owners have. Most won't cover you, and if they do, it's worse than useless. One hundred dollar coverage doesn't help anybody.

Save your money until you expand into that house. Then insure adequately.

Shipping

Remember we talked about that phone in your house and the yellow pages advertisement? Here's a story about shipping ... and that phone I advised you to get.

I had a call from Albuquerque, New Mexico. The gentleman told me that it was his wife's birthday and that on his last trip through DFW (Dallas-Fort Worth) airport he had come into Grapevine to kill a few hours between flights. During a visit to my shop he had seen a Flow Blue plate and a small ashtray. Did we still have them?

Within the next two days, I received his check for $250 and an extra amount of $25 for fourth day ground shipping. I made an extra $19 on the handling, and you should too if you give the service.

I got another order from this gentleman besides! Goes to show how valuable that phone number is. Get yourself a phone number even if all you rent to start with is one booth. Get some business cards printed and leave them in a prominent place in your booth. Never turn down extra business.

I have shipped small items all over the U.S. I have also shipped a washstand to Chicago (in two separate pieces, it only just fit the measurements used by most parcel services), and a pair of iron gates to Macon, Georgia.

It's worth the effort. I know it's a nuisance, but it leads to other sales.

Carry bags

Part and parcel of the antique business. No pun intended. I would suggest you get nice ones. Ask the mall owner to use them for your sales only. If they won't, they won't. It's worth asking. They give your booth its own personality.

Signs

If you do layaway, put up a sign. Many malls recognize that this is part of sales and arrange to take care of it for you. They do not chase the payments, that's up to you. Although all payments are made at the counter, it helps to put up a sign saying that you accept Visa, Mastercard, etc. Customers hate having to go all the way up to the sales counter in a large mall to find out. Never forget that if they pick up that vase, candlestick, etc., and then go to the sales counter, they have bought it. If they have to go up to the sales counter first to find out if credit cards are acceptable, they might not come back to your booth.

Here's a tip: On the layaway sign put your phone number (there it is again!) so that a customer can call you. A sale may hinge on it.

Chapter 15 review

1. **Restoring antiques is no fun unless you have loads of patience**. Don't get into it unless you absolutely have to. Do clean, stain out marks, and wax the pieces to make them look like a million dollars. Get yourself an emergency cleaning and repair bag.

2. **Lamp rewiring is worth it for a few lamps at a time**. Do not end up with lots of them in your garage tying up your hard earned cash.

3. **Taping down lids on teapots**, soup tureens, and other porcelain smalls will save you money and arguments.

4. **Delivery—don't do it until you expand**. When you do, get yourself a man like Rex. The extra dollars earned from deliveries help pay for that special weekly dinner out.

5. **Do not worry yourself into an early grave about theft**. You've costed for it in the 2.5 multiple. And none of that macho stuff please! Many thieves carry guns!

6. **Insurance is usually impossible** and if you can get it, too expensive. Once you expand, get it and insure adequately.

7. **If you ship, your business will grow**. Do it. Put up a sign that says that you ship out of state. The phone number helps.

8. Your own **personalized carry bags** are a nice touch. Ask the mall if they will pack your goods in them.

9. **Signs** help a customer decide to buy and prevent them from getting irritated. If you take credit cards, say so up front. It helps make up the customer's mind.

This was a funny chapter. Bits 'n' Pieces just about sums it up.

16. Do's 'n' Don'ts

Which is more important? Do's or Don'ts?

Maybe both.

As with bits 'n' pieces, many of the things we will cover in this part of the book will be very obvious. Obvious that is, once they are brought to your attention. Some of the don'ts are my pet peeves and I know that at least one will draw a large amount of dissension, since most dealers do it. I have covered it before, but feel that it is important enough to raise once again. Since I am a reckless character, let's start with that, shall we?

Markdowns

A don't in my book. I mentioned this before in Chapter 7. By markdowns, I mean the standard practice of crossing out the original amount on the price tag and simply writing in the reduced price next to it. This method of generating sales is used extensively in discount stores. I don't agree with it in the antique business.

"But it must work," I hear you say, "or else dealers wouldn't do it so often."

Yes, but I believe that it only influences a very small portion of the buying public. Very few dealers try my alternative because it's so much more work to rewrite the tag than it is to cross out the old price and write in a reduced one. If you don't believe me, go to the most successful large antique dealer in your town and see how seldom they cross out prices on the same tag.

So what is my way? I'm sure you'll remember, but I'll tell you again anyway. It's based on my belief that we all want to feel special.

In my opinion, it is far better to redo the tag and write in a new price together with something like this: "Due to the imminent arrival of new incoming stock, I am able to offer this very beautiful occasional table at a highly competitive price of ... " or "Due to an advantageous buying situation I am able to offer this very beautiful ... etc."

I have several reasons why crossing out prices and simply rewriting in new ones is such a bugbear with me:

1. The antique business is considered special and good customers shy away from cheap, used items. We already carry that "junk" impression with seventy percent of the buying public. Let's not add to it.

2. The customers that buy because of the lowball offer will try to knock you down even more.

3. I don't think antiques sell because of price. They sell because of individuality and suitability.

Having said all the above, the only time I would think that showing the markdowns this way would work, is if you are selling really low-end products. More and more antique dealers are getting away from this segment of the market because these are the most problematical customers, and the secondhand stores are much too competitive.

Here is an example that illustrates why I hate scratching out original prices on price tags so much.

For three weeks a customer had been seriously looking at a wonderful, pine curio cabinet. I had it marked at $3000. After seeing it in my store, she went shopping and found a similar piece in Fort Worth. Although not anywhere as nice, it cost less than mine. Still, the quality and design of my unit haunted her. She made an offer of $2000, which I rejected. Five days later, she called and asked what was my lowest price? I told her $2900. "Too much for me," she said, "but I love it. It's the best one I've seen."

Three days later she called again. "Would I go any lower?" she pleaded.

Twenty eight hundred and that's it, I told her.

"I just don't have that much," she replied.

Okay. How about paying me the $2000 you have and the balance of $800 over two months, I offered, and as an added incentive, I will let you take it as long as you give me two postdated checks for the balance.

"I'll come in and talk to you about it," was her reply.

The next day she came in. By the time she left, I had a cash check for $2700 in my sweaty little hand! After I cashed it, I delivered the unit and did not charge her the $30 delivery fee.

Can you imagine what I would have had to come down to if I had already crossed out the price and written a lower one in on the tag?

The point is, if they want it, they will negotiate with you. Don't cut yourself off from dropping the price on a face-to-face basis. It usually closes the sale and makes the customer feel very special because you really care.

Finally, I have this piece of advice: Try both methods. Tell me which works best for you. If my method does, you'll buy me a beer, if yours does, I'll buy you a glass of wine.

Open house days/Cheese and wine parties

A very definite do in my book. Well worth doing at least four times a year. It is really effective when you have expanded into a co-op, but it can also be highly advantageous when done in a booth for a small select group. Saturday morning is the best day for this and coffee and cookies are more appropriate than cheese and wine. Once you are in a co-op or in your own store it becomes easier to administer. This is how I run mine:

Well ahead of time, I choose a Friday and Saturday on which there are no major conflicting events. Do not select the day of the Super Bowl!

Taking my register, I mail out special (note the word special) invitations to my best customers, i.e. those that have bought expensive pieces. This invites them to a cheese and wine get-together on a Friday evening between 6 and 8 p.m. The time is very important because most people then feel that they can come and go on their way to another function. Do not RSVP the invitation because they must feel that they are free to just pop in.

At the same time as sending out this invitation, I mail out flyers to the general public in the area around my business. It invites them to the same open house on Saturday, at which I serve cheese and wine as well as coffee and cookies. Note the subtle use of the different wording.

Why do I change the wording from cheese and wine party to open house?

If you remember the word "special," well done. I change it because I don't want my special customer who couldn't make it on Friday night to pop in on Saturday and think that their special invitation was a load of hogwash.

"What is the purpose of an open house then?"

Obviously to sell, but it's much more than that. Its purpose is to stamp your personality on your business. After all, businesses are all the same—cold, impersonal, and inert. The difference is the owner and his or her relationship with the customer. That's what makes them keep coming back to you.

During an open day function at your booth or co-op, circulate among the customers, talk to them, and give them the attention they deserve. Believe me, they want to know you and when they do, they will come back to buy.

Sometimes I feel that I know my customers almost as much, if not better, than their families do. I certainly know their homes as well as some of their children do, what with today's youth being so much on the go. One lady in particular has been an excellent client. She bought a buffet, a large oil picture, and recently, a beautiful French armoire in mahogany. Due to her busy schedule, we delivered it late one evening. Putting it together in her bedroom reminded me of why I feel these special relationships are so important. Not only was it great fun, but after her husband and I had assembled it, we visited and discussed high school football, golf, and the lighting in her house. Great fun! Incidentally, it looked fabulous in a light peach and flower decor.

Open house days at your booth or co-op are excellent relationship builders. They lead to increased business and more money, money, money! Hold them as coffee and bun days in your booth, or cheese and wine parties in a co-op or shop setting.

Customer is always right!

This is a do—with one exception. Always listen to your customer and if they do have a complaint, bend over backwards to sort it out. Too many dealers don't pay enough attention to this.

Remember, most customers are genuine and only want to feel that you care. A little attention will go a long way.

There is one exception. Every now and then you will get a customer that is totally unreasonable. It's usually because they couldn't afford what they bought. Not only will they ask you to fix one thing, but they will keep finding fault, hoping you will refund their money. At such a time you will have to stand firm, but do it head up and use plain, polite language. As I write this, the vision of a particular curio cabinet keeps floating before my eyes. The gentleman that bought it owns a fast-food business—you would think that he would know better.

It was just before Christmas and he needed a present for his wife. The curio cabinet was a real nice one. Curved glass at the front, a mahogany frame and a red patterned mirror at the back made it one of the most interesting I have ever had. And therein lay the problem. The red pattern clashed with his wife's china.

After negotiation, I agreed to buy a plain new mirror for him to put in the back of the cabinet at an extra cost of $40. Since it was Christmas, the mirror store was closed and he decided to take the unit, give it to his wife, and come back to pick up the mirror after the holidays. All agreed, he and I loaded it into the back of his Honda Civic, during which he damaged a corner. Quickly I pointed this out to him and he agreed that it was his fault.

A week after Christmas, I came into the store to find the unit there. I had called him to pick up the mirror, but during my absence he had dropped off the curio cabinet, telling my assistant that I had agreed to fit it. That was totally untrue. Placed in the cabinet to one side was a secondhand interior light. While calling him to point out that I had not agreed to fit the new mirror, he got extremely irritated and told me that he was just an ordinary customer and that I was the antique expert who knew how to do it. At this stage I was still thinking "the customer is always right" and agreed to do it for $20 extra.

Two weeks later his wife pulled up in a Cadillac. She strode in, looked at the unit, and asked why the light was to one side and not in the center. She was extremely abrasive. Still I held my tongue and just then her husband walked in, which was a mistake. She turned on him and berated him about the light, at which he turned on me and said, "You're the expert, why didn't you move it into the center?"

In this case, the customer was not right.

They left with the unit and I have never seen them again.

Ninety-nine times out of one hundred it is better to try to please the customer. It builds a reputation for caring. When it becomes impossible, state your case straight up and forget that customer. If he comes back, it'll be good business. If not, don't waste your time.

Window cleaner on porcelain

This is a definite don't. Window cleaner takes off the painting on old porcelain. It is far better to use hot water with a little liquid soap, let the piece soak, and then use a soft toothbrush.

I once bought a Dresden carousel. When I picked it up from a dealer in the back of a parking lot, it was covered with grease and looked like hell. It had obviously been kept above the stove in a kitchen. The dealer had been very ill and needed the money to pay his medical bills, so I was able to get this unusual piece for only $650. Taking it home, I soaked it in a mild mixture of warm water, liquid soap, and a touch of vinegar. It took hours, but using a soft toothbrush, it cleaned up beautifully without damaging any of the gilt or color. When clean, it looked like a million dollars! I sold it for $2500 and it looks absolutely terrific in the English oak curio cabinet that the buyer also bought.

When in doubt use liquid soap, warm water, and a touch of vinegar to clean any delicate piece. A definite "do."

Distress repairs

A do and a don't.

Occasionally you will have to add a small corner section or bracket to an old antique. One that comes to mind in my case was an old Welsh buffet. It was a lovely piece—all dark, old glass panes with the twirls in the middle, and more than a few cigarette burns on its character-filled surfaces.

The only problem was that it had an angled corner support missing. Not a big one, but just enough to be noticeable. The question was, do we repair it or leave it alone?

Repair it, was the decision, so I had a piece cut to fit, stained, and matched up. Then we did the "do." We distressed the wood by scratching it, denting it with a wooden club, and rubbing in some fine dust. Waxed over, it looked so original that even I couldn't tell the difference from the one on the other side.

When a customer bought that character-filled dark oak Welsh buffet, I told him about the corner.

"Why did you do that?"

Because he bought a genuine antique of great value and needed to be told. **Do** distress the addition to make it fit in with the character of the piece, and **do** tell.

It all depends on you, but I believe that if you are truly a professional you will be honest. Learn how to distress the wood by practicing as often as you can.

Antique furniture must be the only product that you can sell as original after beating it with a wooden club!

Breaking habits

A very strange don't.

I've put it in for a reason though. As you go about your successful business day in, day out, week in, week out, you will tend to settle into a pattern. It will be easier not to change out the booth this week. "I'll do it next week," you'll tell your wife. "Okay," she will reply, "I'll polish the furniture then, not now."

Don't get complacent. It's very easy to do. You won't notice it until your sales start to drop off.

Always treat your business as if you were just starting. It will make it interesting for you and your customers. Your sales will continue to stay up and you will get a reputation for being an expert. Don't let up on your own standard of quality.

Credit

Don't give it!

Except to your very, very best customers, whom you have known over a very, very long time. My aluminum French cross is an example. An exceptional item, it came from Lourdes in France. How many do you ever get like that? Not many, I can tell you. If you see any, please buy them for me. I'll pay you well!

Mildred, my wonderful customer, wanted it. She had just been on vacation to Europe and all her credit cards were maxed out. I let her take it and accepted that she would pay me the next month. My trust was not misplaced and was based on sound professional judgment. Remember that I told you at the beginning of this book that you have to take chances sometimes. This was one of those times. I should have also added that although human beings are the strangest creatures that walk on God's earth, they are also surprisingly dependable.

Don't give credit ... unless it's Mildred, Donna, Jeanie, and a very select few.

Chapter 16 review

1. **Markdowns that have prices scratched out. Yuk!** Many dealers will disagree with me. You make up your own mind but before you do, try both ways.

2. **Open houses**, whether coffee and cookies in your booth on Saturday, or wine and cheese over the week-end, are great for injecting your personality into your business. Customers love them. **Do it once a month.**

3. **Customers are always right**. Bend over backwards to please, but not for ones that want your arm and your leg!

4. **Window cleaner should only be used on windows and mirrors**. Warm water, liquid soap and a touch of vinegar are better on porcelain.

5. **Do distress repairs, and do tell the customer.**

6. **Don't lose your enthusiasm** and get complacent. Treat every day as if it was your last. Change everything, act as if it was your first day in the antique business and you will enjoy it.

7. **Don't give credit** ... unless it's to ....

$$\$\ \$\ \$\ \$\ \$$

The next chapter is about due. It's about being professional and deals with my opinion on the future of the antique business.

17. Looking Ahead

What do you think of when you look at your future in the antique business? Do you see tremendous growth? Do you see a stagnation? Or do you see an exciting business evolving and changing through many twists and turns like I do? If you do, what form will the industry take in the future, and what will you have to do to keep prospering in it?

Have you ever seen a report on what the future holds for the antique business?

"No."

Neither have I, and the reason is that the industry is too new and too fragmented for anyone to have studied it in detail. I am therefore going to take the plunge. Here is my opinion on what is going to happen in the future. All I ask is that you don't take me too literally and make up your own mind on much of what I say.

Antique malls

These will continue to proliferate for a few years more. We are still in the growth stage, although we are reaching the apex of the heady upward curve. This is hiding a fundamental problem.

"Which is?"

Too many suppliers are chasing too few customers already.

"Why do you say that?"

Because we are already beginning to see the first booth holders dropping away due to making little or no profit. This critical factor is being obscured by the influx of new dealers still entering the business. You can see it in the number of malls that have a "Booth space available" sign in the window. You can also see it in the low prices being obtained by auctioneers for "auction quality merchandise."

I have the advantage of traveling to England every six to eight weeks and talking with the suppliers of English antiques. Most of the English antiques auctioned in the United States are the property of the supplier in England. All the U.S. auctioneer does is auction the goods on their behalf, take his auctioneer's cut, and send the balance back to England. In my recent visits, the English suppliers were making noises about the dropping prices and I have heard some even say that they are considering discontinuing the shipping of goods.

"That's really scary, particularly as I am just getting started."

No, it isn't. It's a time of great opportunity.

"Why's that?"

Because as a professional operator making coldly logical decisions, you will be selling better quality goods for which there is always a market, and you will be buying them at better prices, as other less efficient dealers get rid of merchandise.

"Please explain what you think I should do."

Firstly, stick to top quality merchandise. Secondly, get really tough on the prices you are prepared to pay. Thirdly, keep changing out your booth and making it really interesting, and finally, stick to the very, very unusual.

If you follow the above advice, you will prosper and increase your business while the dealers selling cheap products will find it a struggle.

There is one further thing to watch. Keep a very sharp eye on what's going on in your mall. Listen closely and watch. Are the owners still there all the time? Do you see bill collectors at the desk? Do you detect panic, to the point of desperation, to get in all the booth rents?

If you do, draw back on your commitment and quietly ask if things are tough. If yes, how tough? Be sympathetic and the owner may take you into his confidence. Don't renew your lease except on a month-to-month basis. Start looking elsewhere for new space.

Stick to the very, very unusual. This is a 1760 chatelaine used by housekeepers to keep homes in order. It has a pin cushion, knife holder, missing scissors case, mother-of-pearl perfume bottle, thimble, and tape measure.

Just remember this: Tough times mean greater opportunities for those who are professionally organized. That's you, isn't it?

This is what I think is going to happen in the next few years:

1. The growth will continue, but more slowly.
2. Malls will start having a tougher time attracting dealers and customers. Many will go out of business.
3. Those malls that recognize the oversupply now developing will institute new ways of drawing customers. You will see more entertainment, such as authors signing antique books, talks on antiques by experts, antique musical instrument entertainment, restoration demonstrations, and even free giveaways and free drawing contests being organized. Successful antique malls will become both retail outlets and entertainment centers.

   You don't believe me? Just look at the book business. It's going through the same growing pains and getting much better at selling books by entertaining people at the same time.
4. Dealers selling better quality merchandise will still command good prices and prosper. The really good ones, such as you, will even expand as rents go down. You will become more substantial operators through consolidation.
5. There will be fewer dealers numerically, but they will rent the same amount of booth space. They will also cooperate with each other much more closely.
6. I expect the above to take about three years and then the antique business will resume its upward growth, although at a slower rate.

It's going to be an exciting time! There will be many changes and increased rewards for you and me. Look forward to them.

"I see that. Please go over what you think I should do one more time."

Right. Here goes.

---

1. Buy only top quality merchandise.
2. Fight hard for low prices.
3. Look for really unusual pieces only.

4. Keep an eye on what's going on in your mall. Be prepared to move to one you see coping better with the
   expected downturn. Entertainment is the coming
   thing! Make sure you are surfing with the wave!
5. Work harder at pleasing your customers.
6. Take chances and expand if you see the right opportunity.
7. Watch your overhead like a hawk! Discipline yourself to run your business with your head, not your
   heart.
8. Maintain your profit level. Don't cave in by lowering
   prices. If you have the very unusual, customers will
   pay your prices because they recognize quality and
   can't get it anywhere else.
9. Give service, service, and more service!
10. Look for the active and aggressive dealers in your
    mall and work closely with them.

As I write this I'm really excited. You should be too. Opportunities will abound, and those of us who tackle the future with determination and an entrepreneurial spirit will reap great rewards. The antique business will come out of the stone age and into the space age!

$ $ $ $ $

Since I anticipate a dip in customer demand, it follows that there will also be changes in the ancillary industries servicing the antique business. This is what I think will happen to them.

Auctions

There will be fewer of them. Many auctioneers will turn to other merchandise. This will be no problem for you. You will pick and choose only the best merchandise and get it at better prices.

Sales by other dealers

You will have a field day! There will be lots on offer and at very good prices. Be very, very, picky and make low offers. If they don't take them, move on. There will be lots more where that came from.

Newspaper offers

Same as above, even more so. I expect the lists of merchandise for sale to grow longer as dealers begin to try to sell their merchandise from their garages. Good business for the papers! Also for you. You are going to be a buyer and will have lots to choose from.

Garage sales

More good quality merchandise will become available, but only from ex-dealers. Watch the mall notice board—they will be putting up sale offers and details of their garage sales.

$ $ $ $ $

As you can see from the above comments, I am thrilled about the future. The antique business will go through a shakeout and become much healthier. Those with verve and guts will seize the opportunities and prosper mightily. Those who don't will fall by the wayside. I think that you fall into the former category. Think of it this way:

In the near future you will walk into your mall. The place will be full. In one corner there will be a speaker discussing seventeenth century antiques. In the other a musical group is playing old tunes. Customers will be everywhere—at the snack bar, at the author's signing, and at your beautifully laid-out booths. Best of all, they will be buying your unusual, pretty, and very profitable merchandise! Won't you feel proud?

If you have already expanded into a house, your co-op will be doing the same thing. Come to think of it, you might just steal a march on the whole industry and do that in the next few months. Can you see how special your customers will feel if they are invited to a Friday night discussion on antiques with a visiting expert?

Enough of the chatter. You are going to be a leader in this industry and have work to do.

Chapter 17 review

1. **There is going to be a shakeout**. Inefficient dealers will fall by the wayside, as will old-thinking malls. Many will close.

2. The antique business will become more **customer-oriented**.

3. **Malls will become retail outlets and entertainment centers** at the same time.

4. **A larger percentage of the general buying public will be introduced to antiques** through the entertainment aspect of the industry. There will be more mixing of genuine antiques and good modern interior decorating accessories.

5. **Dealers like you will seize the opportunities**. Through efficiency you will become bigger operators, more professional in your approach, and far, far wealthier. You will definitely make money from antiques.

6. **The antique business will become one of which we will all be proud**.

$$\$ \ \$ \ \$ \ \$$$

Can I be a bit presumptuous here and offer some personal advice?

Don't let the coming shakeout bother you. Ignore the gnashing of teeth and crying of tears as inefficient dealers give up. It is a time of great opportunity. Look to the greater goal and seize it with your entrepreneurial spirit. The future in the antique business will make good dealers very rich.

Let one of them be you.

Look forward!

18. Being Professional

We have come full circle together.

Now we meet as two, mutually respecting professionals. I may still know a little more about the antique business than you do, but not much. Both of us will never know it all, and both of us will have different tales to tell in the future.

This chapter, being the last, will cover my ideas on what being professional means. If there were more professionals, the whole antique business would improve to the benefit of all that love it and make their living from it. I have only to look at my friends in Village Treasures to see how we can all improve to better the industry and to increase our income. It can be a highly profitable business for you. Make it so.

Being a professional antique dealer

"I have my own antique business."

Yes. By now you do. But you also have something else. You have responsibility.

Responsibility to the antique business as a whole, responsibility to your customers, responsibility to your suppliers, but more than anything else, you have responsibility to yourself. You owe it to yourself to succeed and to make money. In doing so, your success will be a result of your professionalism, not a result of your overcharging, cheating, or pure luck. There is no shame in making a profit. There is only shame in making a profit at the expense of others who are not getting fair value. For example:

There is no shame in paying $650 for a grease-caked Dresden porcelain carousel that is so grubby you cannot tell if all the painting is even there. After all, you are taking the risk that the gilt paint is so damaged by the grease that it will flake off once you try to clean it.

Nor is there any shame in selling the beautifully clean and shiny Dresden carousel for $2500. After all, if you check the valuation books you will see that is fair market value. Now that it's in such good condition, your customer is getting a first class, value-for-money piece.

So make your profit. It is your professionalism that led you to take a chance at possibly losing $650 and it is your professionalism and knowledge that allowed you to clean the carousel and bring out its timeless beauty. You deserve to be paid for that.

Feel good about yourself. You have every right to do so.

Being professional also brings other responsibilities. For example:

How many of us write out a code of ethics by which we do business? Not many, that's for sure. And how many of us send a customer to another dealer on the off chance that he may have something our customer is seeking? Now I know that I told you to make money on this by asking the other dealer for a small commission first, but that is only if you know that he has the item and not just on the off chance. In this case, being professional means giving the customer your business card and introducing him/her to another dealer. It will pay dividends later on when the dealer reciprocates.

How about dress code? How often have you gone into a mall to be taken aback at being stared at by an untidily dressed young man who shuffles out from behind the counter in shower sandals and torn shorts? Not only that, he usually has a dirty tee shirt on! I have seen it, and I certainly don't think that's being professional. Even if it's a boiling hot Sunday afternoon, you should at least dress respectfully, and I do think tidy shorts, clean socks, and white sneakers are acceptable.

Now here's another good example of being professional. Write out your refund policy and put it up in your booth. Not only will it make you look professional, it will also save you money.

While you are about it, put up a sign saying that all sales are final, if that is your policy. It will save you arguing with the customer that comes into your booth on a busy Saturday afternoon and demands a refund on the Victrola that he bought four weeks ago. Just by looking at it, you can see that he has worn it to death by playing it a hundred times.

Professionalism means smiling. Smiling at the mall owner, at your customers, and at the auctioneer.

Finally, being a professional antique dealer is a state of mind. If you are proud of your industry, proud of your own business, and proud of being part of a wonderful group of people, it will show.

Which brings me to you.

Thank you for reading this book and bearing with me. I hope you have learned a lot, had fun, and are enjoying running your own antique business. Welcome to the club. You will be a great addition.

Now for one final section. It's as important as any that I have written. I have added it because it is a lesson I am still learning.

Change! Identifying it, managing it, and coping with it

Change is constant—more so in the antique business. Trends come and go, economic climates improve and degenerate, and tastes and incomes governing individual customer's buying abilities change.

Watch for change! Are the cheaper pieces not selling as well as before? Are the more expensive pieces doing better? Are neither doing well? Are small item sales increasing?

Stay on top of your business. Keep an open mind and look at the overall picture, not at the day-to-day one. Take a long-term look.

"How do I do this?"

By listening. Listening and then acting! Listen when other dealers are talking, listen when you go into other malls, and listen when you go into the neighboring stores. Those sources you used when starting your booth are still there, and just as important, if not more so. The salesman in the regular furniture shop is still as interested in talking to you on a quiet Thursday afternoon as he was in the beginning. He will tell you what's happening, particularly as you are now his friend.

Listen, listen, and listen while you ask, ask, and ask again!

So what do you do with all this information? Weed out the individual comments, decide if the customers are getting cautious in their spending and then act on it.

"By doing what?"

If times are getting tough, pull back on purchases of big, expensive furniture and increase your purchases of small decorative pieces. It's a known fact that the gift and entertainment industries do better in tough times than in good ones. People still want to pamper themselves, they just don't have as much money to do it with. They will increase their buying of small crystal vases, nice pictures, and mirrors, while holding back on the big wardrobe.

Conversely, it works in the opposite direction when times are good. Take advantage of this. Good times are for making the bigger profits needed to carry you through the lean times that are surely coming. Buy and sell those expensive French armoires and gilt mirrors now! They make you larger profits than the smaller occasional tables and there are more customers for these when times are good.

Here I've come full circle again. Change is constant. Change is also good ... but only if you pick up on it, alter your merchandise, and offer what is appropriate for the times. It's a bit like summer and winter, right? It's called knowing your market. Managing change is part and parcel of your new professionalism. Don't be afraid of it. Use it to make more money!

$$\$ \ \$ \ \$ \ \$$$

Sometime in the future when you ride around in your new car and reflect on how you started your own antique business, you will wonder how on earth you could have had any doubts. I hope that my experience and knowledge will play some small part in your success. And succeed you will. Trust me.

I will leave you with this thought. **You are going to travel first class!**

I will see you there.

INDEX

A

B

C

D

E

F

M

N

O

P

V

W

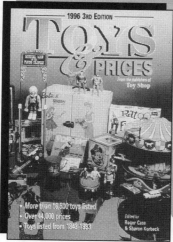

purchasing budget for 20,000 sales target. = 8,600

2.5 mark up